Reading Comprehension and Skills: Grade (

Table of Contents

Printed in the USA • All rights reserved.

ISBN 978-1-60418-258-3

Ready-to-Use Ideas and Activities

This book was developed to help students master the basic skills necessary to become competent readers. The stronger their foundation in reading basics, the faster and easier students will be able to advance to more challenging texts.

Mastering the skills covered within the activity pages of this book is paramount for successful reading comprehension. The activities at the beginning of the book aim to build and reinforce vocabulary, the foundation of reading comprehension. These activities lead to practice with more advanced comprehension skills such as categorizing and using context to understand words.

All students learn at their own rate; therefore, use your judgment to introduce concepts to students when developmentally appropriate.

Hands-On Learning

Hands-on learning reinforces the skills covered within the activity pages and improves students' potential for comprehension. One idea for a hands-on activity is to use the removable flash cards at the back of this book to play a game of bingo. To do this, make a copy of the bingo card (page 3) for each student. Write the flash card words on the board and have students choose 24 of the words and write them in the empty spaces of their bingo cards in any order. When students have finished writing on their cards, gather the flash cards into a deck. Call out the words one at a time. Any student who has a word that you call out should make an *X* through the word on their card to cross it out. The student who crosses out five words in a row first (horizontally, vertically, or diagonally) wins the game by calling out, "Bingo!" To extend the game, continue playing until a student crosses out all of the words on their bingo card.

Comprehension Checks and Discussion

In addition to the activities in this book, support reading comprehension growth by reading stories in the classroom. After a story—or part of a story—is read, ask your students questions to ensure and enhance reading comprehension. The first type of question you might ask is a factual question. A factual question includes question words such as *who, what, when, where, how,* and *why.* For example, *How old is the character?, Where does the character live?, What time was it when. . .?,* or any other question that has a clear answer. You might also ask open-ended questions. These types of questions do not have a clear answer. They are based on opinions about the story, not on facts. For example, an open-ended question might be *Why do you think the character acted as he did?, How do you think the character felt about her actions or the actions of others?, What do you think the character will do next?,* or *What other ways could this story have ended?* As students learn to think about these questions as they read, they will retain more of the material and understand it at a higher level.

 CD-104308 • © Carson-Dellosa

Vocabulary Bingo

		FREE		

Name _____

Greek and Latin Roots

Many English words contain roots from other languages such as Greek and Latin. For example, the word *monarch* contains the roots *mon*, meaning "one," and *arch*, meaning "ruler." Therefore, a *monarch* is "one ruler," or a person who rules a country alone. Read the list of roots below.

bio: life	**ast:** star	**zoo:** animals	**geo:** earth
psych: mind	**archaeo:** ancient	**bot:** plant	**anthrop:** human

Use these roots to help you match the following words with their meanings.

archaeologist	zoologist	psychologist	biologist
anthropologist	botanist	astronomer	geologist

1. scientist who studies plants _____

2. scientist who studies the human mind _____

3. scientist who studies ancient people _____

4. scientist who studies different life forms _____

5. scientist who studies the earth _____

6. scientist who studies human cultures _____

7. scientist who studies the solar system _____

8. scientist who studies animals _____

 CD-104308 • © Carson-Dellosa

Greek and Latin Roots

Many English words contain roots from other languages such as Greek and Latin. For example, the word *thermometer* contains the roots *therm* and *meter*. *Therm* means "heat," and *meter* means "to measure." Therefore, a *thermometer* is a device that measures heat. Read the list of roots below.

dent: tooth	**cardi:** heart	**neur:** nerve	**pod:** foot
hemo: blood	**ped:** child	**opt:** eye	**derm:** skin

Use these roots to match the following words with their meanings. Write the correct word in each blank.

cardiologist	hematologist	dermatologist	pediatrician
ophthalmologist	neurologist	podiatrist	dentist

1. doctor who examines blood _____

2. doctor who examines feet _____

3. doctor who examines children _____

4. doctor who examines teeth _____

5. doctor who examines the nervous system _____

6. doctor who examines skin _____

7. doctor who examines the heart _____

8. doctor who examines eyes _____

Name _____

Greek and Latin Roots

Many English words contain roots from other languages such as Greek and Latin. For example, the word *semicircle* contains the roots *semi* and *circle*. *Semi* means "half," so a *semicircle* is half of a circle. Read the list of roots below.

mille: thousand	**poly:** many	**centi:** hundred	**quad:** four
tri: three	**hemi:** half	**equi:** equal	**oct:** eight

Use these roots to match the following words with their meanings. Write the correct word in each blank.

polygon	triangle	centimeter	hemisphere
octagon	quadrilateral	millisecond	equivalent

1. figure with many sides _____

2. having equal measure _____

3. figure with three sides _____

4. half of a sphere _____

5. figure with four sides _____

6. $\frac{1}{100}$ of a meter _____

7. figure with eight sides _____

8. $\frac{1}{1,000}$ of a second _____

 CD-104308 • © Carson-Dellosa

Greek and Latin Roots

Many English words contain roots from other languages such as Greek and Latin. For example, the word *bicycle* contains the roots *bi* and *cycl*. *Bi* means "two," and *cycl* means "a circle or ring." Therefore, a *bicycle* is a vehicle that has two circles, or wheels. Read the list of roots below.

omni: all	**nutri:** nourish	**herba:** grass	**spir:** breathe
phys: body, nature	**carn:** meat	**aero:** air	**chlor:** green

Use these roots to help you match the following words with their meanings.

herbivore	nutrition	physical	respiration
aerobic	carnivore	chlorophyll	omnivore

1. something that makes plants' leaves green _____

2. animal that eats only plants _____

3. taking in the food necessary for health and growth _____

4. the act of breathing _____

5. animal that eats only meat _____

6. helping the body take in more oxygen _____

7. relating to the body _____

8. animal that eats all kinds of food _____

Name _____

Greek and Latin Roots

Many English words contain roots from other languages such as Greek and Latin. For example, the word *submarine* contains the roots *sub* and *marine*. *Sub* means "below," and *marine* means "water." Therefore, a *submarine* is a vehicle that travels below the water. Read the list of roots below.

ann: year	**auto:** self	**loc:** place	**chron:** time
dem: people	**fac:** make	**spec:** see	**biblio:** book

Use these roots to match the following words with their meanings.

democracy	bibliography	location	chronology
factory	spectator	anniversary	autobiography

1. place where things are made _____

2. position of something _____

3. date marking a yearly event _____

4. person who watches something _____

5. list of events in order _____

6. book about a person's own life _____

7. government by the people _____

8. list of reference books _____

Greek and Latin Roots

Many English words contain roots from other languages such as Greek and Latin. For example, the word *television* contains the roots *tele* and *vision*. *Tele* means "distance," and *vision* means "to see." Therefore, a *television* is an object that lets you see things from a distance. Read the list of roots below.

cred: believe	**jud:** law	**crypt:** hidden	**temp:** time
mar: sea	**leg:** read	**aud:** hear	**port:** carry

Use these roots to match the following words with their meanings.

audible	temporary	credible	marine
cryptic	judicial	legible	portable

1. able to be carried _____

2. relating to the law _____

3. relating to the sea _____

4. able to be believed _____

5. lasting for only a short time _____

6. able to be read _____

7. mysterious _____

8. able to be heard _____

Greek and Latin Roots

Many English words contain roots from other languages such as Greek and Latin. For example, the word *monorail* contains the roots *mono* and *rail*. *Mono* means "one," so a *monorail* is a vehicle that runs on a single rail. Read the list of roots below.

cap: take, seize	**brev:** short	**ver:** truth	**magn:** large
nomen: name	**alter:** other	**nov:** new	**cogn:** know

Use these roots to match the following words with their meanings.

alternate	recognize	abbreviate	magnify
novice	nominate	verify	captivate

1. to be familiar with _____

2. to make larger _____

3. to hold someone's attention _____

4. to make shorter _____

5. to change between two things _____

6. to make sure something is true _____

7. to name someone as a candidate for office _____

8. someone who is new at doing something _____

Greek and Latin Roots

Many English words contain roots from other languages such as Greek and Latin. For example, the word *international* contains the Latin root *inter*. *Inter* means "between," so something that is *international* happens between nations. Read the list of roots below.

mater: mother	**quer:** ask	**ped:** foot	**onym:** name
aqua: water	**frater:** brother	**arch:** leader	**pater:** father

Use these roots to match the following words with their meanings.

aquatic	monarch	paternal	pedometer
fraternal	query	antonym	maternal

1. motherly _____

2. one ruler _____

3. device that measures footsteps _____

4. brotherly _____

5. having to do with water _____

6. word that means the opposite _____

7. question _____

8. fatherly _____

Compound Words

Compound words are two words that have been joined to form another word. They do not always keep the meanings of both words. For example, a *skyscraper* does not actually scrape the sky. A *skyscraper* is a very tall building. In the chart below, write the literal meaning for each word that makes up the compound word. Then, write what the compound word means.

Compound Word	Literal Meaning for First Word	Literal Meaning for Second Word	Actual Meaning
1. airport			
2. jellyfish			
3. newspaper			
4. upstairs			
5. playground			
6. bookkeeper			
7. waterfall			
8. birthday			
9. popcorn			
10. afternoon			

Name _____

Compound Words

Compound words are two words that have been joined to form another word. They do not always keep the meanings of both words. For example, a *turtleneck* sweater is not actually worn over the neck of a turtle. A *turtleneck* sweater is a sweater that covers your neck all the way to your chin. In the chart below, write the literal meaning for each word that makes up the compound word. Then, write what the compound word means.

Compound Word	Literal Meaning for First Word	Literal Meaning for Second Word	Actual Meaning
1. tiptoe			
2. blueprint			
3. bedspread			
4. rainbow			
5. quicksand			
6. shoelace			
7. backyard			
8. suitcase			
9. cattail			
10. toothbrush			

Compound Words

Compound words are two words that have been joined to form another word. They do not always keep the meanings of both words. For example, a *brainstorm* does not actually mean "a storm occurring in the brain." A *brainstorm* is when you think of a lot of ideas for solving a problem. In the chart below, write the literal meaning for each word that makes up the compound word. Then, write what the compound word means.

Compound Word	Literal Meaning for First Word	Literal Meaning for Second Word	Actual Meaning
1. uproot			
2. airplane			
3. whirlpool			
4. shortstop			
5. haircut			
6. clothespin			
7. postcard			
8. supermarket			
9. teacup			
10. sailboat			

CD-104308 • © Carson-Dellosa

Compound Words

Compound words are two words that have been joined to form another word. They do not always keep the meanings of both words. For example, an *anchorperson* is not a person who carries an anchor. An *anchorperson* is a person who reads news stories and introduces other news reporters on television. In the chart below, write the literal meaning for each word that makes up the compound word. Then, write what the compound word means.

Compound Word	Literal Meaning for First Word	Literal Meaning for Second Word	Actual Meaning
1. buttercup			
2. underground			
3. sandpaper			
4. downtown			
5. fireplace			
6. pancake			
7. sidewalk			
8. carpool			
9. grasshopper			
10. haystack			

Name _____

Compound Words

Compound words are two words that have been joined to form another word. They do not always keep the meanings of both words. For example, *frostbite* does not actually mean "being bitten by the frost." When you have *frostbite*, part of your body feels frozen from cold weather. In the chart below, write the literal meaning for each word that makes up the compound word. Then, write what the compound word means.

Compound Word	Literal Meaning for First Word	Literal Meaning for Second Word	Actual Meaning
1. paperback			
2. earthquake			
3. football			
4. lighthouse			
5. thumbprint			
6. necklace			
7. bookcase			
8. storeroom			
9. breakfast			
10. boxcar			

 CD-104308 • © Carson-Dellosa

Name _____

Compound Words

Compound words are two words that have been joined to form another word. They do not always keep the meanings of both words. For example, something that is *offbeat* is not actually off the beat. Something that is *offbeat* is unusual or out of the ordinary. In the chart below, write the literal meaning for each word that makes up the compound word. Then, write what the compound word means.

Compound Word	Literal Meaning for First Word	Literal Meaning for Second Word	Actual Meaning
1. grandmother			
2. paintbrush			
3. software			
4. partnership			
5. earring			
6. scarecrow			
7. sunshine			
8. armchair			
9. overcoat			
10. strawberry			

Shortened Words

Some words are shortened forms of longer words. For example, the word *ad* is short for *advertisement*. Read the sentences below. Fill in each blank with a word that is a shortened form of a word in the word box.

mathematics	airplane	telephone	refrigerator	veterinarian
influenza	gymnasium	teenager	draperies	examination

1. We put our leftovers in the _____ when we got home from the restaurant.

2. My stepdad took our dog to the _____ because he needed a vaccination.

3. Lauri flew in a _____ to her granddad's house in another state.

4. Every year, my mom gets a shot to make sure she does not get the _____.

5. Our basketball team practices after school in the _____.

6. Last night, I completed five pages in my _____ book.

7. My sister just turned 13, so she is a _____ now.

8. Marisa said that she needed to make a _____ call.

9. Next week, we have an _____ in science class.

10. Grandma wants to put up new _____ in her living room.

Shortened Words

Some words are shortened forms of longer words. For example, the word *wig* is short for *periwig*, a word that is no longer used by most people. Read the sentences below. Fill in each blank with a word that is a shortened form of a word in the word box.

luncheon	omnibus	necktie	automobile	champion
gasoline	memorandum	tuxedo	taxicab	popular

1. Some songs are part of _____ culture.

2. My uncle took a _____ to the airport so that he could leave his car at home.

3. Theo is the _____ on his soccer team.

4. We will eat _____ at noon.

5. The groom wore a _____ to his wedding.

6. I ride the _____ to and from school.

7. The principal sent out a _____ to all of the teachers.

8. Dad wears a _____ with a nice shirt when he goes to work.

9. Sylvie's mom stopped at the _____ station on the way home.

10. Grandpa took his car to an _____ mechanic.

Name _____

Shortened Words

Some words are shortened forms of longer words. For example, the word *mart* is short for *supermarket*. Read the sentences below. Fill in each blank with a word that is a shortened form of a word in the word box.

dormitory	saxophone	bicycle	rhinoceros	graduate
laboratory	representative	limousine	photograph	submarine

1. Mom took a _____ of my brother and me on our first day of school.

2. Lan plays the _____ in the school band.

3. Manuel wants to be our class's _____ on the student council.

4. The _____ has a large horn.

5. My cousin is now a college _____.

6. Pamela rides her _____ to school.

7. A _____ takes people deep below the ocean's surface.

8. Susie's older brother lives in a college _____.

9. A scientist often works in the _____.

10. My older sister and her friends took a _____ to their school dance.

 CD-104308 • © Carson-Dellosa

Name _____

Shortened Words

Some words are shortened forms of longer words. For example, the word *clerk* is short for *cleric*, a word that is no longer used by most people. Read the sentences below. Fill in each blank with a word that is a shortened form of a word in the word box.

chimpanzee	logogram	hamburger	gemstone	condominium
technical	videotapes	biography	carbohydrates	delicatessen

1. My cousins and I like to watch old _____ of our parents' childhoods.

2. The _____ near our house serves delicious sandwiches.

3. The company's _____ has two blue stars inside a red circle.

4. When the computer would not work, Mom called for _____ support.

5. Aunt Edna lives in a new _____ downtown.

6. I enjoyed reading the _____ of Queen Elizabeth.

7. Juan would like a _____ with his fries.

8. We saw a _____ named Freddy in the old movie.

9. Protein and _____ are different kinds of food.

10. The _____ in Greta's ring sparkled in the sunlight.

Portmanteau Words

Portmanteau words were made by combining two words. For example, the word *brunch* was made by combining *breakfast* and *lunch*. Make a new word by combining the words in each row to make a word in the word box. Then, write what the new word means.

camcorder	flare	moped	glimmer	motel	smog
motorcade	crunch	splatter	spork	fanzine	sitcom

1. flame + glare = _____ meaning: _____

2. smoke + fog = _____ meaning: _____

3. motorcar + parade = _____ meaning: _____

4. crispy + munch = _____ meaning: _____

5. motor + hotel = _____ meaning: _____

6. spoon + fork = _____ meaning: _____

7. gleam + shimmer = _____ meaning: _____

8. splash + spatter = _____ meaning: _____

9. camera + recorder = _____ meaning: _____

10. fan + magazine = _____ meaning: _____

11. motor + pedal = _____ meaning: _____

12. situation + comedy = _____ meaning: _____

Synonyms

Synonyms are words that have nearly the same meaning. Read the sentences below. Choose the word in the word box that is a synonym for the boldfaced word. Then, write it on the line below the sentence.

considered	told	increase	threatened	critical
document	billfold	collecting	empty	

1. The storyteller **narrated** the tale in a deep, booming voice.

   _____

2. I received a **certificate** that said I had successfully completed the course.

   _____

3. The mayor said that providing funding for the hospital was an **urgent** issue.

   _____

4. The judge **contemplated** the evidence before making her decision.

   _____

5. That house has been **vacant** for several months.

   _____

6. Dad took a $10 bill out of his **wallet** and handed it to the clerk.

   _____

7. The habitat of many animals is **endangered**.

   _____

8. My uncle has been **accumulating** baseball cards since he was a child.

   _____

9. The large speakers **amplify** the volume of the music.

   _____

Synonyms

Synonyms are words that have nearly the same meaning. Read the sentences below. Choose the word in the word box that is a synonym for the boldfaced word. Then, write it on the line below the sentence.

bendable	achieve	quick	greatest	bright
cautiously	feed	hobby	forceful	

1. Grandpa likes to wear shirts with **vivid** colors when he plays golf.

   _____

2. The children's toy is made out of **flexible** plastic.

   _____

3. My favorite **pastime** is painting pictures of flowers using watercolors.

   _____

4. Mom **gingerly** opened the door to find out where the noise was coming from.

   _____

5. If you work hard, you can **attain** any goal.

   _____

6. The announcer told us in an **emphatic** voice that the train was about to depart.

   _____

7. The **maximum** number of students in a class at my sister's school is 22.

   _____

8. It is important to **nourish** your body with healthy foods.

   _____

9. Cherie walked across the room with a **brisk** stride.

   _____

Synonyms

Synonyms are words that have nearly the same meaning. Read the sentences below. Choose the word in the word box that is a synonym for the boldfaced word. Then, write it on the line below the sentence.

peaceful	spines	nimble	slight	eagerness
beautiful	certain	confused	exact	

1. The weather forecaster said that there was only a **scant** chance of rain.

   _____

2. I was **perplexed** by the math problem at first, but then it began to make sense.

   _____

3. The pond was very **tranquil** at sunset.

   _____

4. Rita's gold necklace is **exquisite**.

   _____

5. We were asked to give a **literal** translation of the Spanish phrase.

   _____

6. A hedgehog's **bristles** help protect it from predators.

   _____

7. Our coach felt **confident** that we could win the game.

   _____

8. The gymnast was very **agile** on the balance beam.

   _____

9. Abel has a great **fervor** for learning and spends every Saturday at the library.

   _____

Synonyms

Synonyms are words that have nearly the same meaning. Read the sentences below. Choose the word in the word box that is a synonym for the boldfaced word. Then, write it on the line below the sentence.

well-known	ridiculous	isolated	weak	struggled
imitate	external	objective	confirmed	

1. Ted felt **frail** after his illness last winter.

   _____

2. My **intention** is to finish my homework before dinner.

   _____

3. The **outward** appearance of the library may look old, but there are many new books inside.

   _____

4. Marita wore an **absurd** costume in the play.

   _____

5. The teacher **certified** that the grades were correct.

   _____

6. Frieda's uncle lives in a **secluded** house in the country.

   _____

7. Dad **grappled** with the shutters before he finally closed them.

   _____

8. Professor Wu is an **eminent** scholar.

   _____

9. My little brother likes to **mimic** a cat when we are playing.

   _____

Synonyms

Synonyms are words that have nearly the same meaning. Read the sentences below. Choose the word in the word box that is a synonym for the boldfaced word or phrase. Then, write it on the line below the sentence.

admiration   occupied   occupation   jostle   description
pleasant   blanket   delicate   see

1. Ginny is always **cordial** to visitors who come to her house.

   _____

2. My brother wants to pursue the **profession** of firefighting.

   _____

3. The **caption** under the painting said that it was painted in 1752.

   _____

4. We have great **awe** for her talent as a pianist.

   _____

5. That antique vase is very **fragile**.

   _____

6. Uncle Roy had to **push and shove** the door to get it to close tightly.

   _____

7. The meadow near my house is **inhabited** by rabbits and mice.

   _____

8. We could barely **perceive** our house through the fog.

   _____

9. Aunt Cathy sewed a **quilt** from fabric scraps.

   _____

Name _____

Synonyms

Synonyms are words that have nearly the same meaning. Read the sentences below. Choose the word in the word box that is a synonym for the boldfaced word. Then, write it on the line below the sentence.

matching	globe	loyalty	predict	continually
enthusiasm	area	knickknacks	tools	

1. Mandy is **perpetually** in a good mood.

   _____

2. Earth is a **sphere** that orbits the sun.

   _____

3. My sister's room is decorated with **trinkets** from other countries.

   _____

4. Leah said to drop in for a visit if we were in her **vicinity**.

   _____

5. Dad bought new cooking **utensils** when we moved to a new apartment.

   _____

6. She has so much **excitement** for football that she attends every game.

   _____

7. Kimberly and her cousin have **identical** sweaters.

   _____

8. Some meteorologists try to **forecast** the weather.

   _____

9. Lupe is known for her **fidelity** to her friends.

   _____

Synonyms

Synonyms are words that have nearly the same meaning. Read the sentences below. Choose the word in the word box that is a synonym for the boldfaced word. Then, write it on the line below the sentence.

unbiased	products	previous	liquids	lift
chime	exciting	decorated	stylish	

1. When you are ill, you should drink plenty of **fluids**.

   _____

2. We paid for our **merchandise** and left the store.

   _____

3. The bells **peal** every day at noon.

   _____

4. The referee gave us her **neutral** opinion about which team had scored the point.

   _____

5. Grandpa wears a **jaunty** hat when he goes to a parade.

   _____

6. It took five people to **hoist** the couch into the truck.

   _____

7. We took an **exhilarating** ride on the roller coaster.

   _____

8. Sometimes we receive mail for our home's **former** occupant.

   _____

9. The store window was **ornamented** with lights and ribbons.

   _____

Name _____

Antonyms

Antonyms are words that have opposite meanings. Read the sentences below. Choose the word in the word box that is an antonym for the boldfaced word. Then, write it on the line below the sentence.

slower	dull	afterword	maximum	absent
bought	different	before	depleted	

1. The **minimum** charge for admission to the play is $3.

_____

2. My two brothers look very **similar**.

_____

3. Depending on the weather, I may be **present** for the hike tomorrow.

_____

4. The dance team practices **after** school.

_____

5. The horse's gait grew **faster** when the rider gave it the command.

_____

6. Grandma **sold** her house last year.

_____

7. Mom wants to paint our living room in **vivid** colors.

_____

8. The snack tray was **replenished** halfway through the party.

_____

9. The **foreword** told why the author wrote the book.

_____

Antonyms

Antonyms are words that have opposite meanings. Read the sentences below. Choose the word in the word box that is an antonym for the boldfaced word. Then, write it on the line below the sentence.

smooth	old	gloomy	depreciate	tranquil
final	simple	near	common	

1. Gene's face was **radiant** after the game ended.

   _____

2. The salesperson asked whether we were looking for anything **special**.

   _____

3. The cafeteria was very **hectic** at lunchtime.

   _____

4. Some animals have very **rough** fur.

   _____

5. My brother can see objects that are **far** away with his new glasses.

   _____

6. The coach's **initial** thought was that the team would win the game.

   _____

7. The quilt in my room has an **elaborate** design on one side.

   _____

8. When you invest money, sometimes it will **appreciate**.

   _____

9. Many people are looking to use **new** sources of energy.

   _____

Antonyms

Antonyms are words that have opposite meanings. Read the sentences below. Choose the word in the word box that is an antonym for the boldfaced word. Then, write it on the line below the sentence.

young	lengthen	calm	found	urban
giant	excludes	rigid	unusual	

1. Some people **abbreviate** their names.

   _____

2. Our teacher said that the exam schedule was **flexible**.

   _____

3. Nancy's little sister **lost** her ball.

   _____

4. A **typical** Saturday activity for me is running in the park with my mom.

   _____

5. Someday I would like to live in a **rural** area.

   _____

6. Our math homework **involves** fractions and decimals.

   _____

7. The store was **lively** on the day before the holiday.

   _____

8. Uncle Vic baked **miniature** cupcakes for the bake sale.

   _____

9. I played the game with my **elderly** uncle.

   _____

Multiple Meanings

Many words have more than one meaning. The way a word is used in a sentence can help you figure out which meaning is being used. Read the sentences below. Choose the correct meaning of the boldfaced word or phrase as it is used in the sentence. Then, circle the letter of the correct meaning of the word or phrase.

1. The engineers were afraid that the bridge would **buckle** under too much weight.
   a. piece of metal worn in the middle of a belt
   b. collapse or give way under pressure

2. The committee will **deliberate** on the issues.
   a. discuss before making a decision
   b. done on purpose after careful consideration

3. Amie **chimed in** with her ideas for the bake sale.
   a. interrupted or added to the discussion
   b. rang to indicate the time

4. The mayor's popularity **soared** after her speech.
   a. flew high into the air
   b. rose sharply

5. Dad **pried** open the door to the shed.
   a. interfered with someone's personal business
   b. forced apart with a lever

6. Please **relay** my message to the principal.
   a. communicate or pass along to
   b. race with a team of runners

7. We **scoured** the park for the clues to the mystery.
   a. scrubbed clean
   b. searched thoroughly

8. A **plume** of smoke rose from the chimney.
   a. feather of a bird
   b. long column or band

Multiple Meanings

Many words have more than one meaning. The way a word is used in a sentence can help you figure out which meaning is being used. Read the sentences below. Choose the correct meaning of the boldfaced word as it is used in the sentence. Then, circle the letter of the correct meaning of the word.

1. We tried to **prod** him into joining the team.
   a. urge someone on
   b. nudge or poke sharply

2. Deanna's **rash** decision caused her to lose the game.
   a. hasty or reckless
   b. skin inflammation

3. Mom paid a **toll** when we crossed the bridge.
   a. ring like a bell
   b. small tax or fee

4. Jared could not **fathom** how his team had won the game.
   a. depth of six feet (1.8 m)
   b. come to understand

5. Her **initial** reaction to the rain was to cancel the race.
   a. first or beginning
   b. capital letter of a name

6. Aunt Ceci will have surgery for a pinched **nerve**.
   a. part of the body
   b. courage or daring

7. The river has a very high **bank**.
   a. a place to keep money
   b. a slope or hill

8. We asked the cashier to **void** our transaction.
   a. cancel
   b. empty space

Multiple Meanings

Many words have more than one meaning. The way a word is used in a sentence can help you figure out which meaning is being used. Read the sentences below. Choose the correct meaning of the boldfaced word as it is used in the sentence. Then, circle the letter of the correct meaning of the word.

1. The representative used her office as a **vehicle** for communicating her views.
   a. type of transportation
   b. means of expression

2. Mom will **cinch** the belt around her waist.
   a. fasten tightly
   b. something certain to happen

3. The farmer made **furrows** in the earth with the plow.
   a. deep troughs to plant crops in
   b. wrinkles in a person's brow

4. My teacher asked me to **condense** my report to one page.
   a. change from vapor to liquid water
   b. make shorter or more compact

5. Anthony's great-grandfather was a **distinguished** professor.
   a. told two things apart from each other
   b. be famous for accomplishments

6. I **skimmed** the material again before the test.
   a. looked at quickly
   b. glided across

7. We were asked to **refrain** from talking during the assembly.
   a. avoid
   b. repeated part of a song

8. The city's new development **sprawls** over many miles.
   a. lies down
   b. stretches out

Multiple Meanings

Many words have more than one meaning. The way a word is used in a sentence can help you figure out which meaning is being used. Read the sentences below. Choose the correct meaning of the boldfaced word as it is used in the sentence. Then, circle the letter of the correct meaning of the word.

1. To what **degree** do you agree with his remarks?
    a. measurement of temperature
    b. extent of a condition

2. I could not **contain** my enthusiasm about my new bicycle.
    a. enclose in a jar
    b. keep under control

3. The director **posted** the results from the audition for the play.
    a. a pole set up to mark something
    b. to announce publicly

4. My first **impression** of my new school was that I liked it very much.
    a. feeling
    b. imprint

5. The tapestry has **elaborate** designs on it.
    a. detailed or complex
    b. tell more about

6. The map has a **legend** to tell us what the symbols mean.
    a. story told from the past
    b. explanation of symbols

7. The science test was **tough**, but I think I did well.
    a. hard to chew
    b. difficult

8. I felt **sheer** relief when the swim meet was over.
    a. absolute
    b. transparent

Multiple Meanings

Many words have more than one meaning. The way a word is used in a sentence can help you figure out which meaning is being used. Read the sentences below. Choose the correct meaning of the boldfaced word as it is used in the sentence. Then, circle the letter of the correct meaning of the word.

1. The fisherman told a funny **yarn** about life at sea.
   a. thick thread used for knitting
   b. tale that is hard to believe

2. The bike shop charges a **flat** rate for replacing tires.
   a. set or not varying
   b. smooth and even

3. Last year, my father learned how to **operate** a computer.
   a. use the controls on
   b. perform surgery

4. The tree branch **grated** against the window.
   a. irritated
   b. scraped

5. Mom said that my new sunglasses **suit** me.
   a. look appropriate on
   b. matched set of clothing

6. Scientists say that Earth's **core** is very hot.
   a. set of basic classes
   b. innermost part

7. The candidate might **flounder** if someone asks about an unfamiliar issue.
   a. struggle for words
   b. type of fish

8. We are planning a trip to **scale** that mountain.
   a. climb or rise gradually
   b. device used for weighing

Name _____

Vocabulary

Multiple Meanings

Many words have more than one meaning. The way a word is used in a sentence can help you figure out which meaning is being used. Read the sentences below. Choose the correct meaning of the boldfaced word as it is used in the sentence. Then, circle the letter of the correct meaning of the word.

1. The U.S. president's **cabinet** must be approved by the Senate.
   a. wooden cupboard
   b. council of advisors

2. Grandma **grilled** vegetables for dinner.
   a. cooked over a fire
   b. questioned intensely

3. That antique painting has **appreciated** over time.
   a. increased in value
   b. felt grateful for

4. A good education is **critical** for success later in life.
   a. disapproving
   b. important

5. The banker deposited $500 in the **vault**.
   a. piece of gymnastic equipment
   b. large safe

6. We enjoyed the **sparkling** conversation at the party.
   a. glittering
   b. interesting

7. Reyna put the horse in the **stall** after she groomed him.
   a. area of a barn
   b. halt or pause

8. Matthew thought of a **novel** approach to solving the problem.
   a. new or innovative
   b. fictional book

38

CD-104308 • © Carson-Dellosa

Definitions

Read the sentences below. Use the context clues to figure out the definition of each boldfaced word. Then, write the letter of the correct definition on the line.

a. to show how

b. people who move from another country

c. decision

d. made shorter

e. plans

f. able to be changed

g. provide nutrients

h. usually

i. mechanical device

j. forecasted

1. The word *doctor* can be **abbreviated** as *Dr.* _____

2. Ms. Yang **demonstrated** how to complete the experiment. _____

3. My brother and I **typically** spend each summer at our grandmother's house. _____

4. The sportscaster **predicted** that the visiting team would win the game. _____

5. My **schedule** includes activities every day after school. _____

6. The coach asked us to keep our plans **flexible** in case our team made the playoffs. _____

7. Eating a variety of foods helps to **nourish** the body. _____

8. My mother's parents were **immigrants** from Russia. _____

9. Mom fixed the **mechanism** so that she could move the garage door up and down. _____

10. The judge said that she had reached a **verdict**. _____

Definitions

Read the sentences below. Use the context clues to figure out the definition of each boldfaced word. Then, write the letter of the correct definition on the line.

a. a part played by an actor
b. at the edge
c. common saying
d. left out
e. characteristics of a surface

f. satisfied
g. at the same time
h. pull out
i. took back
j. stages

1. My uncle used a hammer to **wrench** the nail out of the board. _____

2. Daniel tried out for a **role** in the school play. _____

3. Silk has a very smooth **texture**. _____

4. Our class called out the answer to the question in **unison**. _____

5. I **retrieved** my hat from the lost-and-found box. _____

6. We learned about the **phases** of the moon in science class. _____

7. Tony **quenched** his thirst after the race by drinking water. _____

8. The scientists believed that they were on the **verge** of finding a cure for the disease. _____

9. An old **maxim** is "A stitch in time saves nine." _____

10. The teacher accidentally **omitted** Cathy's name from the list. _____

Definitions

Read the sentences below. Use the context clues to figure out the definition of each boldfaced word. Then, write the letter of the correct definition on the line.

a. small fragment of something
b. first or at the beginning
c. area around and including a city
d. someone speaking
e. to inspire

f. small printed paper
g. feeling or guess
h. does well
i. put into action
j. speaks nonsense

1. My **initial** impression was that soccer was a difficult game, but I soon changed my mind. _____

2. The **narrator** of the documentary spoke in a very soft voice. _____

3. The volunteers passed out a **pamphlet** listing ways people could help clean up the environment. _____

4. We will try to **implement** our new plan next week. _____

5. I have a **hunch** that it will snow tomorrow. _____

6. Mom is good at **motivating** me to do well in everything I try. _____

7. She thought she had found the missing puzzle **piece**. _____

8. Last year, we moved from a rural area to a **metropolitan** region. _____

9. Candace **excels** at math and science. _____

10. Joey's little sister is learning to talk, but right now she **babbles**. _____

Definitions

Read the sentences below. Use the context clues to figure out the definition of each boldfaced word. Then, write the letter of the correct definition on the line.

a. large meeting

b. calm or relaxed

c. school grounds

d. do well

e. to convince

f. live in

g. manner of speaking

h. brought together

i. large dish

j. liquid to drink

1. Laura spoke with a foreign **accent** as part of her character in a play. _____

2. There was a guest speaker on **campus** last week. _____

3. My favorite **beverage** is lemonade. _____

4. My mom was out of town last month at a **convention**. _____

5. Lydia is a **serene** person who never raises her voice. _____

6. Please put the fruit slices on the serving **platter**. _____

7. The sisters were **reconciled** after 10 years. _____

8. Some plants **thrive** in rocky soil. _____

9. A diverse range of people **inhabit** our town. _____

10. We tried to **coax** Max into playing the fiddle for us. _____

Definitions

Read the sentences below. Use the context clues to figure out the definition of each boldfaced word. Then, write the letter of the correct definition on the line.

a. put forward   **f.** pushed by bumping
b. not well-known   **g.** in part
c. manner of walking   **h.** to begin or start
d. wool   **i.** noticed
e. book about a person's life   **j.** figured out

1. Our assignment is to write a summary of a **biography**. _____

2. Mia **asserted** her opinion at the meeting. _____

3. Please take your seats because the presentation is about to **commence**. _____

4. We **deduced** the answer to the problem. _____

5. The topic of her report is an **obscure** painter from the Middle Ages. _____

6. My project is only **partially** complete. _____

7. Amanda has a very fast **gait**, so it is hard to keep up with her. _____

8. My arm was **jostled** when someone tried to move past me in the crowd. _____

9. The science teacher asked us to write everything we **perceived**. _____

10. The sheep's **fleece** was thick. _____

Definitions

Read the sentences below. Use the context clues to figure out the definition of each boldfaced word. Then, write the letter of the correct definition on the line.

a. full of detail
b. hurried
c. the study of words
d. to take care of immediately
e. pledge of assurance

f. list of food options
g. to be careful with something
h. driving force
i. think ahead
j. makes wrinkles

1. In our language arts class, we are learning **grammar**. _____

2. Dad **furrows** his brow when you ask him a tough question. _____

3. The **menu** lists seven different sandwiches. _____

4. Caleb drew an **intricate** design on the mural. _____

5. The mayor says that the city must be **prudent** with its money. _____

6. I like to **speculate** about what career might be in my future. _____

7. Mom said that it is **urgent** that I clean my room because Granddad is coming to visit. _____

8. The store offered a **guarantee** that it would fix any problems that occurred within the first 30 days after purchase. _____

9. Our team had enough **momentum** after the first half to win the game. _____

10. Aunt Faye **bustled** around getting ready to leave the house. _____

Definitions

Read the sentences below. Use the context clues to figure out the definition of each boldfaced word. Then, write the letter of the correct definition on the line.

a. exactly like

b. leave out

c. a document written by hand

d. breakfast food made from grain

e. quieted down

f. shiny surface

g. someone who helps

h. introduction

i. breathtaking

j. thought about

1. The potter put a special **glaze** on her mugs and bowls. _____

2. When I looked down at my shoes, I realized that my socks were not **identical**. _____

3. The librarian showed us a rare **manuscript** from the fourteenth century. _____

4. The view from the mountaintop was **exhilarating** after the long climb. _____

5. My dad **pondered** my question for a long time before answering. _____

6. The chatter **subsided** as the speaker walked onto the stage. _____

7. Our reading club does not **exclude** anyone who loves to read. _____

8. The author explained the book's purpose in its **preface**. _____

9. Timothy is my best **ally** on the team; we work together well. _____

10. I often eat a bowl of **cereal** before I go to school. _____

Definitions

Read the sentences below. Use the context clues to figure out the definition of each boldfaced word. Then, write the letter of the correct definition on the line.

a. the same as
b. tradition
c. to be very different
d. deep thinking
e. handwritten names

f. at the edge or onset
g. abundant, luxurious
h. member of a profession
i. friends
j. to plan to do something

1. Due to decreased sales, the business is on the **brink** of bankruptcy. _____

2. Our family **custom** is to go to Grandma's house for New Year's Eve. _____

3. Erin and I have been best **pals** since first grade. _____

4. One foot is **equivalent** to 12 inches. _____

5. In the school play, I wore an **outlandish** hat with a giant flower. _____

6. If it snows, someone on the school's **faculty** will contact the TV station about canceling school. _____

7. Michaela **intends** to enroll in medical school after college. _____

8. The club hung **lavish** decorations for the banquet. _____

9. That book makes a **profound** statement about the world today. _____

10. Some people have elaborate **signatures** with many swirls. _____

Definitions

Read the sentences below. Use the context clues to figure out the definition of each boldfaced word. Then, write the letter of the correct definition on the line.

a. to ask questions   **f.** dried
b. threw away   **g.** revealed in secret
c. wonder   **h.** conditions
d. charming   **i.** restored confidence
e. type of poetry   **j.** made louder

1. Grandma **assured** me that I would perform better in the next game. _____

2. I **queried** the teacher because I did not understand the project requirements. _____

3. Shakespeare was known for his 14-line **sonnets**. _____

4. We watched the professional basketball players and were in **awe** at their skill. _____

5. It was not clear under what **circumstances** Dad would be needed at the office over the weekend. _____

6. Amelia **discarded** her sandwich wrapper. _____

7. I **raised** my voice so that everyone could hear my speech. _____

8. Wendy **confided** that she would try out for the play. _____

9. We brought **dehydrated** apricots for a snack. _____

10. The old-fashioned movie was **enchanting**. _____

Definitions

Read the sentences below. Use the context clues to figure out the definition of each boldfaced word. Then, write the letter of the correct definition on the line.

a. handed out   **f.** not able to be seen
b. watches over   **g.** to move quickly
c. group of sentences **h.** native environment
d. an award   **i.** went before
e. to remember   **j.** to copy or imitate

1. My brother **briskly** raked the leaves so that he could go to the movies with his friends. _____

2. The employee received a **commendation** for her excellent service. _____

3. The teacher **distributed** the worksheets for us to complete. _____

4. A series of advertisements **preceded** the movie. _____

5. In my **recollection**, last summer was a lot of fun. _____

6. A lifeguard **supervises** swimmers at a beach. _____

7. Sarita can **mimic** any voice she hears. _____

8. An amphibian's **habitat** is part land and part water. _____

9. Germs are **invisible** without a microscope. _____

10. Your paper should begin with an introductory **paragraph**. _____

CD-104308 • © Carson-Dellosa

Name _____

Read the story. Then, answer the questions.

Hammurabi's Code

One reason that modern countries run smoothly is that their laws are published. Because of this, all citizens know what laws they must follow. During ancient times, laws were not always recorded. A Babylonian king named Hammurabi created the first set of written laws for his people around 1760 B.C.E. He wanted to bring all of the people in his empire together under one set of laws. Because the laws were written down, everyone, whether rich or poor, was expected to obey them. Hammurabi's Code included 282 laws written in cuneiform, a type of writing in which symbols were carved into clay tablets. Each law included a penalty, or punishment, for disobeying it. The laws were written on a stela, which was a large slab of stone that was posted for all to see. Archaeologists working in the area now known as Iran discovered the stela in 1901. Spectators may view Hammurabi's Code in the Louvre Museum in Paris.

1. What is the main idea of this story?
    a.   Modern countries publish their laws.
    b.   Hammurabi's Code was an ancient set of laws.
    c.   Archaeologists often find ancient materials.

2. Who was Hammurabi?

    _____

    _____

3. Why did Hammurabi write down his laws?

    _____

    _____

4. Where were Hammurabi's laws written?

    _____

5. Where did archaeologists find Hammurabi's Code?

    _____

Name _____

Read the story. Then, answer the questions.

Athens and Sparta

Athens and Sparta were two important city-states in ancient Greece. A city-state is a region controlled by one city that is usually part of a larger cultural area. The citizens of both Athens and Sparta were ruled by elected assemblies. In addition, Athens had elected leaders called archons, while Sparta had kings who governed until they died or were overthrown. The people of Athens valued education and the arts and sciences. However, the people of Sparta focused on military life. Men in Sparta had to serve in the military from a young age, while men in Athens could choose whether to serve or not. The Greek city-states fought each other during the Peloponnesian War, from 431 to 404 B.C.E. Although Sparta defeated Athens, it was conquered later by the city of Thebes. Today, the city of Sparta is remembered for its military skill. In contrast, Athens is remembered for its philosophers and writers.

1. What is the main idea of this story?
   a. The city of Thebes was also located in Greece.
   b. Sparta's kings ruled until they died or were overthrown.
   c. Sparta and Athens were two very different city-states in ancient Greece.

2. What is a city-state?

   _____

   _____

3. How were the governments of ancient Athens and Sparta different?

   _____

4. How were the governments of ancient Athens and Sparta similar?

   _____

5. What is Athens remembered for today?

   _____

CD-104308 • © Carson-Dellosa

Name _____

Read the story. Then, answer the questions.

Alexander the Great

Alexander the Great was the son of a Macedonian king. He was born in 356 B.C.E. Alexander learned about Greek culture from his teachers, including the famous philosopher Aristotle. Alexander became king at age 20, when his father died. He spread the Greek culture to foreign areas covering over 22 million square miles (nearly 57 million square kilometers). Alexander was an unusual ruler because he allowed people in different areas to govern themselves as long as they followed Greek customs. Alexander's empire shared a common currency and language, and many cities were named Alexandria in his honor. People from different parts of the empire, such as the Middle East and India, began to share knowledge with each other. This led to great achievements in science and art. Alexander died at age 33, and his empire was split among three generals. Alexander's empire was later absorbed into the Roman Empire.

1. What is the main idea of this story?
    a. Alexander the Great was an important leader in ancient times.
    b. Alexander was the son of a Macedonian king.
    c. Aristotle was a great philosopher of ancient Greece.

2. How did Alexander learn about Greek culture?

    _____

3. What made Alexander an unusual leader?

    _____

    _____

4. What similarities did parts of Alexander's empire share?

    _____

    _____

5. What happened to Alexander's empire after his death?

    _____

    _____

Read the story. Then, answer the questions.

The Tang Dynasty

For many years, China was governed by a series of dynasties, or rulers from the same family. The Tang Dynasty, which ruled from about 618 to 907 A.D., is considered China's Golden Age. Theater, dancing, sculpting, and painting were all very popular during this time. The capital city, Chang'an, had over one million people. Farmers were allowed to own land, although this later changed. People who wanted to work in the government had to pass a difficult exam. Only the smartest and most educated people could serve as government officials. The Tang government took a census to determine the empire's population, and households paid taxes on grain and cloth. Trade inside China and to other countries flourished because new roads and waterways made it easier to travel. Today, the Tang Dynasty is seen as a time of great cultural achievement.

1. What is the main idea of this story?
    a. The Tang government taxed grain and cloth.
    b. The Tang Dynasty lasted for nearly 300 years.
    c. The Tang Dynasty was a period of great cultural achievement.

2. What artistic activities were popular during the Tang Dynasty?

    _____

3. How did people become government officials?

    _____

4. Why did the government take a census?

    _____

5. Why did trade in the Tang period flourish?

    _____

Name _____

Read the story. Then, answer the questions.

The Silk Road

The Silk Road was not really a road, nor was it made out of silk. The Silk Road is the name used to refer to the route leading from Asia to the West. People traveled along this route to trade goods, including silk and spices from China and gold and silver from Rome, Italy. Few people traveled the entire distance of the Silk Road because it was several thousand miles long and very dangerous. The route included deserts and mountains, and there was always the danger of meeting bandits. People traded with each other along the way and took goods with them to others farther along. In addition to goods, ideas and inventions were also traded along the Silk Road. Some technological innovations that travelers brought from Asia to the West included the magnetic compass and the printing press. The Italian adventurer Marco Polo was one of many travelers along the Silk Road.

1. What is the main idea of this story?
    a. Many goods and ideas were traded along the Silk Road.
    b. The Silk Road was long and dangerous.
    c. Marco Polo traveled along the Silk Road.

2. What was the Silk Road?

    _____

    _____

3. What did people trade along the Silk Road?

    _____

    _____

4. Why did few people travel the entire distance of the Silk Road?

    _____

5. What were two technological innovations brought from Asia to the West?

    _____

Read the story. Then, answer the questions.

The Inca Empire

The Inca lived in the Andes Mountains in what is now Peru about 600 years ago. As the Inca empire expanded to include new areas, engineers and workers from the capital city of Cuzco built roads that connected the empire. Government officials recorded the number of people and the amount of wealth in the new areas, and governors were appointed to oversee them. The millions of people living in the Inca empire had to follow the Incan customs, including speaking the Incan language. Cuzco, which had gardens, paved streets, and stone buildings, was located high in the mountains. The city was used mostly for government work and for sending and receiving messages throughout the empire. The emperor and his family lived in Cuzco, but most other people were farmers in the countryside. Although the Inca were defeated by the Spanish in the 1530s, their descendants still live in Peru today.

1. What is the main idea of this story?
   a. The Spanish came to Peru in the 1530s.
   b. The Inca had an impressive empire about 600 years ago.
   c. Cuzco was the capital of the Inca empire.

2. What happened when a new area joined the Inca empire?

   _____

   _____

   _____

3. What did Cuzco look like?

   _____

   _____

4. What activities took place in Cuzco?

   _____

5. What did most people in the Inca empire do for work?

   _____

Name _____

Read the story. Then, answer the questions.

The Trail of Tears

People of different cultures lived in North America before European explorers arrived. As Europeans began to settle the New World, they competed with Native Americans for land and other resources, such as gold. Over time, the New World was divided into states and a government was formed. The U.S. government passed laws in the 1830s making it legal to force Native Americans to relocate if settlers wanted their land. The Cherokee and other Native American groups had to move from the southeastern United States to lands farther west. Thousands of Native Americans traveled over 1,000 miles (1,600 kilometers) on foot from their homelands to the land that later became the U.S. state of Oklahoma. Many people died from disease or hunger along the route. The name "Trail of Tears" was given to this event in U.S. history because of the struggles people faced on their journeys. Today, the descendants of the survivors of the Trail of Tears make up the Cherokee Nation.

1. What is the main idea of this story?
    a. Many people from Europe settled in the New World.
    b. Some Native Americans still live in Oklahoma today.
    c. The Trail of Tears was a forced relocation of Native Americans in the United States.

2. What did European settlers compete with Native Americans for?

   _____

3. How did the U.S. laws that were passed in the 1830s affect Native Americans?

   _____

4. Where were Native Americans forced to move?

   _____

5. What is the Trail of Tears?

   _____

   _____

   _____

Read the story. Then, answer the questions.

The Vikings in Canada

The Vikings were the first Europeans to cross the Atlantic Ocean and reach North America. Historians knew that the Vikings settled in Greenland and Iceland but were not sure how much time they spent in Canada. In 1960, a Viking settlement from around 1000 A.D. was found at L'Anse aux Meadows, in what is now the Canadian province of Newfoundland and Labrador. Archaeologists uncovered the ruins of eight buildings that had sod walls and roofs over supporting frames. In the middle of each floor was a long, narrow fireplace used for heating and cooking. Archaeologists also found tools the Vikings had used. Because the design of the tools and the buildings was similar to those found in Viking settlements in Greenland and Iceland, it was clear that the Vikings settled in Canada as well. Today, L'Anse aux Meadows is a national historic site, and many people visit it each year.

1. What is the main idea of this story?
    a. A Viking group once lived in Canada at L'Anse aux Meadows.
    b. The first Europeans to reach North America were the Vikings.
    c. Many people visit national historic sites each year.

2. In which areas of North America did the Vikings settle?

    _____

3. What was found in 1960 at L'Anse aux Meadows?

    _____

4. What did the buildings at L'Anse aux Meadows look like?

    _____

    _____

5. How did archaeologists know that this was a Viking settlement?

    _____

    _____

Name _____

Read the story. Then, answer the questions.

The Klondike Gold Rush

The Klondike Gold Rush is named after a river where a large deposit of gold was found in 1896. The Klondike River is located near Dawson City in Canada's Yukon Territory. People who wanted to travel from Alaska into Canada in search of gold had to bring a year's worth of supplies with them because there were no places along the way to get more supplies. They often spent time in Edmonton, Canada, stocking up on food, tools, and clothing for the journey. The gold rush helped develop new towns in western Canada and the Pacific Northwest of the United States. In addition to thousands of prospectors, or people who searched for gold, the gold rush drew many professionals, such as doctors and teachers, who were needed in the new settlements. Today, the Klondike Gold Rush International Historical Park, which includes sites in both Canada and the United States, helps people remember the dreams of the prospectors and the difficulties they faced.

1. What is the main idea of this story?
   a. Only a few people became rich during the gold rush.
   b. The Klondike Gold Rush brought many new people to Canada.
   c. Dawson City is located in the Yukon Territory.

2. What is the Klondike Gold Rush named after?

   _____

   _____

3. What did people need to bring with them when traveling from Alaska to Canada?

   _____

4. What did people often do in Edmonton?

   _____

5. Where did new towns develop during the gold rush?

   _____

   _____

Name _____

Read the story. Then, answer the questions.

North American Pioneers

Many early North American pioneers came from Europe. Some came to pursue religious freedom, while others wanted more land for their families. Many settlers built villages along the shores of lakes, rivers, or the ocean. Water was important not only for drinking, farming, and washing clothes, but for powering mills and traveling to other settlements. Most pioneers worked as farmers. They had to clear the land of trees before they could plant many crops. Pioneers also raised horses and oxen to help pull wagons, and sheep to provide wool. When there were enough children in a village, parents sometimes built a schoolhouse and hired a teacher. Usually, all of the children were taught in a single room. Otherwise, children might be educated at home. As villages grew in size, they sometimes built a doctor's office, a blacksmith's shop, and a general store where goods were sold.

1. What is the main idea of this story?
    a. Some pioneers came from Europe.
    b. Pioneer children sometimes studied at home.
    c. Most early pioneers were farmers who lived in small villages.

2. Why did the early pioneers come to North America?

   _____

3. Which animals did pioneers often raise?

   _____

4. How were pioneer children educated?

   _____

   _____

5. What other buildings might a pioneer village include?

   _____

Name _____

Read the story. Then, answer the questions.

New England

Six U.S. states make up the area of New England. Massachusetts was founded in 1630 by people who disagreed with the teachings of the Church of England. The first settlers there were the Pilgrims, who arrived on the *Mayflower* in 1620. Rhode Island was founded in 1636 by people who left the Massachusetts Bay Colony seeking religious freedom. People who settled in New Hampshire, which was founded in 1638, were looking for a place to fish and trade successfully. People who moved to Connecticut, which was founded in 1636, settled on the fertile farmland along the Connecticut River. Maine was once part of the Massachusetts Bay Colony but became a separate state under the Missouri Compromise of 1820. Vermont, founded in 1777, was fought over by several colonies and was originally called New Connecticut. Today, New England is famous for many things, including its beautiful autumn foliage and its fishing industry.

1. What is the main idea of this story?
   a. Many people in New Hampshire enjoy fishing.
   b. Massachusetts was founded in 1630.
   c. New England is a region of the United States.

2. Which states make up the area of New England?

   _____

   _____

3. Why did people settle in Massachusetts and Rhode Island?

   _____

4. What businesses did people in New Hampshire work in?

   _____

5. What is New England famous for today?

   _____

Name _____

Read the story. Then, answer the questions.

Early Industries in North America

One of the earliest industries in North America was the trade of animal fur. Many French explorers who came to the New World in the early 1500s began to trade European goods, such as tools and jewelry, to Native American groups for animal pelts. The French traded furs and other goods around the lakes and rivers of North America. Another important industry was logging. Early settlers of North America had to chop down trees to make room for their farms. In addition to using logs for their own houses, fuel, and furniture, they sold wood to people in other areas to use for paper or durable goods. As farms grew successful, settlers also began to sell goods such as grain and rice. Another important industry in North America was mining. Settlers from Europe found that the New World had many natural resources to mine, such as gold, silver, and precious stones.

1. What is the main idea of this story?
    a. Many settlers used logs to build their houses.
    b. Early North American industries included the fur trade, logging, and mining.
    c. Some early industries are still important today.

2. When did the French explorers come to the New World?

   _____

3. Where did the French trade furs and other goods?

   _____

   _____

4. What goods did settlers begin to sell to people in other areas?

   _____

5. What natural resources did settlers mine in North America?

   _____

Name _____

Read the story. Then, answer the questions.

The Panama Canal

The Panama Canal is a human-made shipping channel that connects the Pacific Ocean with the Atlantic Ocean. This waterway makes it much easier for ships to take goods from one place to another. Instead of traveling around the southern tip of South America, ships can cut through the Isthmus of Panama. An *isthmus* is a narrow strip of land that connects two larger landmasses and has water on its other sides. The Panama Canal was completed in 1914, after 34 years of effort by France and the United States. An estimated 80,000 people worked on the canal before it was completed. The canal works by opening a series of locks, or chambers, through which a ship passes. As the ship enters each lock, the water level slowly rises so that it can safely travel into the next area. Since the canal was built, over 800,000 ships have crossed through it.

1. What is the main idea of this story?
    a. The Panama Canal is a waterway connecting two oceans.
    b. Panama is a country in South America.
    c. Many people worked on the canal before it was completed.

2. How did the Panama Canal change the way ships travel?

    _____

    _____

3. What is an *isthmus*?

    _____

    _____

4. How long did it take to build the Panama Canal?

    _____

5. What do ships pass through on the Panama Canal?

    _____

Name _____

Read the story. Then, answer the questions.

The Smithsonian Institution

The Smithsonian Institution in Washington, D.C., is the largest museum complex in the world. The Smithsonian is named after James Smithson, a British scientist who wanted to create a research institution in the United States. The first structure in the museum complex was built in 1855. Today, the Smithsonian includes 19 museums, nine research centers, and the National Zoo. The National Museum of Natural History has exhibits on plants, animals, human cultures, gems, and ecosystems. The National Air and Space Museum has exhibits on the history and future of flight. The National Zoo has examples of habitats from around the world and works to educate people about protecting wild animals. The Smithsonian also has separate museums devoted to African art, sculpture, portraits of American leaders, folk art and photography, and Native American cultures. An estimated 24 million people visit the Smithsonian each year to see over 136 million objects.

1. What is the main idea of this story?
   a. The first structure in the Smithsonian system was built in 1855.
   b. The Smithsonian is a large museum complex in the United States.
   c. Museums often have exhibits about human cultures.

2. Who is the Smithsonian named after?

   _____

3. How many buildings does the Smithsonian include?

   _____

   _____

4. What type of exhibits does the National Air and Space Museum have?

   _____

5. What other subjects are Smithsonian museums devoted to?

   _____

   _____

   _____

Name _____

Read the story. Then, answer the questions.

Photosynthesis

Photosynthesis is the process in which plants use sunlight to produce food and oxygen. In addition to light, plants need water and carbohydrates to grow. A plant gathers water through its roots. It also takes in carbon dioxide from the air. A compound called chlorophyll helps plants use sunlight. Chlorophyll is what makes plants green. Plants use energy from the sun to break down the water and carbon dioxide. Through photosynthesis, plants produce oxygen and glucose. Glucose is a type of sugar that plants use for energy. Some people refer to trees as the "lungs of the planet." This is because trees help keep a balance between oxygen and carbon dioxide in the air. When people or animals breathe in oxygen, they exhale carbon dioxide. Plants convert carbon dioxide into oxygen that people and animals can breathe.

1. What is the main idea of this story?
   a. People and animals breathe in oxygen.
   b. Plants use energy from the sun.
   c. Photosynthesis is a process that helps plants produce food and oxygen.

2. What do plants need to grow?

   _____

3. What makes plants green?

   _____

4. What is glucose?

   _____

   _____

5. Why are trees sometimes called the "lungs of the planet"?

   _____

   _____

Read the story. Then, answer the questions.

Migration

Some animals migrate, or move, to different areas during different seasons. They may go to warmer climates during the winter and cooler climates during the summer. Some whales swim to Hawaii in the autumn to give birth to their young in warm waters. Then, they travel to Alaska in the summer. Salmon begin their lives in freshwater streams and travel to the ocean as adults. Their bodies change so that they can survive in saltwater. When it is time to lay eggs, salmon swim back to the freshwater streams where they were born. Monarch butterflies fly thousands of miles every autumn, from the northern United States to Mexico. In the spring, they fly north again. Many birds also migrate every year. The arctic tern has the farthest journey, traveling over 22,000 miles (32,000 km) from the Arctic Circle at the North Pole to Antarctica at the South Pole.

1. What is the main idea of this story?
   a. Some animals migrate at different seasons of the year.
   b. The arctic tern migrates over 22,000 miles a year.
   c. Hawaii has warmer waters than Alaska.

2. List one reason why animals might migrate.

   _____

   _____

3. Where do salmon travel during their lives?

   _____

   _____

4. Where do monarch butterflies migrate every autumn?

   _____

5. Which animal has the farthest migration each year?

   _____

Name _____

Read the story. Then, answer the questions.

Fossils

Fossils are the remains of plants or animals from thousands of years ago that have turned to stone. After these organisms died, their bodies were buried in sediment and gradually replaced by minerals. Sometimes an animal's bones, teeth, or shell are preserved. Other times only an impression of its body is made. Footprints, eggs, and nests can also be fossilized. Fossils can be found in many places. They are often uncovered when people dig up the earth as they build roads. Many fossils are buried in layers of rock. Sometimes, fossils are exposed through erosion of a mountainside. Others are found through undersea excavation. Scientists study fossils to learn what the living animals or plants looked like. They can use radiocarbon dating to find out how old a fossil is. All living things contain carbon, so scientists measure how much carbon is left in a fossil to determine its age.

1. What is the main idea of this story?
   a. Fossils can be found in many places.
   b. Sometimes only an impression of a plant is left.
   c. Fossils are plant or animal remains from long ago.

2. What happens when something is fossilized?

   _____

3. What parts of an animal's body might be preserved?

   _____

4. Why do scientists study fossils?

   _____

5. How does radiocarbon dating help scientists determine a fossil's age?

   _____

   _____

Read the story. Then, answer the questions.

Types of Rocks

Rocks are divided into three types, depending on how they were formed. These three types are igneous, sedimentary, and metamorphic. Igneous rocks are made when volcanoes erupt and release melted material called magma. After the magma cools, it forms solid igneous rock. One type of igneous rock is granite, a very hard material that is often used in construction. Sedimentary rocks form when water deposits sediments, or small pieces of rocks and sand. Over time, the sediments are compressed into layers, forming sedimentary rock. One type of sedimentary rock is limestone, which often contains fossils and shells. Metamorphic rocks are the least common of the three types. Metamorphic rocks begin as igneous or sedimentary rocks but are squeezed tightly within the earth's crust over a long period of time. Marble is one type of metamorphic rock.

1. What is the main idea of this story?
    a. Hard rocks can be useful for building sturdy structures.
    b. There are three types of rock that are formed in different ways.
    c. Not all rocks look the same.

2. What are the three types of rock?

   _____

3. How do igneous rocks form?

   _____

   _____

4. How do sedimentary rocks form?

   _____

   _____

5. How do metamorphic rocks form?

   _____

   _____

Name _____

Read the story. Then, answer the questions.

The Beaufort Scale

Wind speed can be measured in miles or kilometers per hour (mph or km/h). A British naval commander in the early 1800s invented a chart called the Beaufort scale to describe the weather using wind speed. Beaufort numbers range from 0 to 12. The number 0 indicates that there is almost no wind, the sea is flat, and the land is calm. In a moderate breeze (number 4), the wind travels at 13–18 mph (20–29 km/h), small waves are present, and small branches begin to move. In a gale (number 8), the wind is moving at 39–46 mph (63–75 km/h), the sea has fairly high waves with breaking crests, and twigs on trees are breaking. During a hurricane (number 12), the wind speed is at least 73 mph (118 km/h), the sea is completely white with foam and spray, and there is massive structural damage on land.

1. What is the main idea of this story?
   a. Wind speed is a rate measured in distance over time.
   b. The Beaufort scale describes weather using wind speed.
   c. Hurricanes can be very destructive.

2. What does the number 0 on the scale mean?

   _____

   _____

3. Describe a moderate breeze on the Beaufort scale.

   _____

   _____

4. What happens during a gale?

   _____

   _____

5. What is the wind speed during a hurricane?

   _____

Name _____

Read the story. Then, answer the questions.

Bird Watching

Many people enjoy the hobby of bird watching. It is a pastime you can do in your own yard. If you put seeds in a bird feeder or hang a birdhouse, you are more likely to attract birds. You may notice that birds visit the feeder at certain times of day, or that different birds prefer different types of foods. You may see baby birds trying their wings as they leave the nest for the first time. Some people travel to other parts of the world to see birds that they cannot see at home. They may use binoculars to get a better look at birds perching in trees or flying overhead. Some people keep lists of the species of birds that they have seen. There are even contests to see who can spot the most different birds over a period of time!

1. What is the main idea of this story?
    a. Bird watching is a popular hobby that many people enjoy.
    b. Some birds like to eat seeds, while others like fruit.
    c. There are many different species of birds.

2. How can you attract more birds to your yard?

    _____

3. What are some things you might notice about birds in your yard?

    _____

    _____

4. What do people use to help them see birds from a distance?

    _____

5. What kind of contest might a bird watcher participate in?

    _____

    _____

Read the story. Then, answer the questions.

Biomes of the World

Biomes are areas of land or water that share the same climate. Earth has several major biomes. Deserts receive little rain and have extreme temperatures. Forests receive more rain and have moderate temperatures. The trees in a deciduous forest lose their leaves every autumn. The trees in the taiga are mostly evergreens, many of which have needle-like leaves. Grasslands cover the most area of land on Earth. Rain is usually seasonal, so there is a dry season during which dust storms may be created. The tundra is located at very high elevations and near the North and South Poles. Few plants grow in the tundra, and the ground is permanently frozen. There are two types of aquatic biomes: marine and freshwater. Marine biomes cover about three-fourths of Earth's surface and include all of the world's oceans. Freshwater biomes are bodies of water such as lakes, rivers, and ponds.

1. What is the main idea of this story?
    a. Some biomes receive little rain.
    b. Deserts can be very hot or very cold.
    c. Earth has many different biomes.

2. What are biomes?

   _____

3. How are deserts and forests different?

   _____

   _____

4. What do many evergreens look like?

   _____

5. What happens during the dry season in the grasslands?

   _____

Read the story. Then, answer the questions.

Energy Conservation

Conserving energy means being careful about how much energy you use and trying to use less energy. You can conserve energy by using cars with higher fuel efficiency, which means you can travel farther using less fuel. You can recycle or reuse materials, such as plastic, glass, paper, and metal, and you can buy products made from recycled materials. You can also conserve energy by using less at home. Wear heavier clothing instead of turning up the heat when the weather grows cooler. Turn off the lights when you leave a room and unplug small appliances and machines such as televisions and computers when you will be away from the house for a long period of time. Using less electricity, gas, and water means you will have lower utility bills and will help the environment.

1. What is the main idea of this story?
   a. Some materials can be recycled instead of thrown away.
   b. Utility bills are sometimes higher in the summer.
   c. There are many ways to conserve energy.

2. What does energy conservation mean?

   _____

   _____

3. Why might you want to use a car with high fuel efficiency?

   _____

4. What are some materials that can be recycled?

   _____

   _____

5. What are two ways to conserve energy at home?

   _____

   _____

   _____

Read the story. Then, answer the questions.

Microscopes

A microscope is a scientific tool that helps people to see very small things. By magnifying tiny objects many times, scientists can view intricate details. Hans and Zacharias Jenssen produced a tube with magnifying lenses at either end in the late 1500s. Anton van Leeuwenhoek developed a single-lens microscope in the mid-1600s. He was the first person to describe bacteria that he saw under the microscope. Early microscopes could magnify objects only up to 20 or 30 times their size, but Leeuwenhoek's device could magnify up to 200 times. Today, scientists use compound microscopes that have multiple lenses to further magnify an image up to 1,000 times. In 1931, two German scientists invented the electron microscope, which can magnify up to one million times. This device directs a beam of electrons at a cell sample to form an image that is captured on a photographic plate.

1. What is the main idea of this story?
    a. Scientists have developed and improved microscopes over time.
    b. Bacteria can be seen under a microscope.
    c. Compound microscopes use multiple lenses.

2. What did the device produced by Hans and Zacharias Jenssen look like?

    _____

3. What was Leeuwenhoek able to describe for the first time?

    _____

4. How has magnification in microscopes changed over time?

    _____

    _____

5. How does an electron microscope work?

    _____

    _____

Read the story. Then, answer the questions.

Potential and Kinetic Energy

Energy is the ability to do work. Energy can be found in the forms of motion, sound, heat, and light. All energy can be classified as either potential or kinetic. Potential energy is stored for later use. Kinetic means "being active," and things using kinetic energy have moving parts. You might think of cogs moving in an engine, but electricity is also an example of kinetic energy because it involves the movement of electrons. Sound and sunlight are also kinetic. Energy can be changed from potential to kinetic. A ball resting at the top of a slope has potential energy. As soon as the ball begins to roll, the energy becomes kinetic. When you are sitting at your desk, you have the *potential* to move. You may store up energy, especially if you sit for a long time. When you begin moving, you become *kinetic*.

1. What is the main idea of this story?
   a.   Energy can be either kinetic or potential.
   b.   Energy can be found in many different forms.
   c.   A group of runners has kinetic energy.

2. What is potential energy?

   _____

3. What is kinetic energy?

   _____

4. How does energy change from potential to kinetic?

   _____

   _____

5. What is an example of kinetic energy?

   _____

   _____

Name _____

Read the story. Then, answer the questions.

Exploring Space

People have been fascinated by outer space for centuries. The first animals sent into space were fruit flies, which traveled on a U.S. rocket in 1947. Many countries sent monkeys into space to investigate how space travel might affect humans. A Russian dog named Laika became the first animal to orbit Earth in 1957. In 1961, the Russian cosmonaut Yuri Gagarin became the first person to travel into space. His spacecraft orbited Earth once and then landed. In 1969, the American astronaut Neil Armstrong became the first person to walk on the moon. The United States developed a space shuttle during the 1980s that could be used many times, like an airplane. Russia built a space station called *Mir* that was used for many years. Astronauts began assembling the International Space Station in 1998. This research station is a cooperative project among many countries, including the United States, Russia, Japan, Brazil, Canada, and 11 European countries.

1. What is the main idea of this story?
    a. People have always been fascinated by outer space.
    b. Space travel has improved greatly over the past several decades.
    c. *Mir* was a Russian space station.

2. Why did many countries send monkeys into space?

   _____

3. Who was the first person to travel into space?

   _____

4. What was significant about the space shuttle?

   _____

5. What is the International Space Station?

   _____

   _____

Read the story. Then, answer the questions.

Constellations

Constellations are patterns of stars that are present in the night sky. Some constellations are named after animals, and others are named after mythical characters. Although stars in a constellation may look close together, they are actually very far apart. Brighter stars are closer to Earth, and dimmer stars are farther away. The International Astronomical Union (IAU) recognizes 88 official constellations. One of the best-known constellations is the Big Dipper. The stars appear to form the handle and bowl of a water dipper. The Big Dipper is part of a larger constellation known as Ursa Major, or the Great Bear. People in different parts of the world see different parts of the night sky. Different constellations are also visible at different times of year. However, some constellations can be seen by people in both hemispheres. For example, the constellation of Orion, the hunter, is visible in both the Northern and Southern Hemispheres, but in the Southern Hemisphere it appears upside down!

1. What is the main idea of this story?
    a.   Constellations are patterns of stars that are present in the night sky.
    b.   Some stars are very far from Earth.
    c.   Australia is located in the Southern Hemisphere.

2. What are constellations named for?

    _____

3. Why do some stars appear brighter than others?

    _____

    _____

4. What is the IAU?

    _____

5. What do the stars of the Big Dipper appear to form?

    _____

    _____

Read the story. Then, answer the questions.

Eclipses

An eclipse happens when Earth and the moon line up with the sun. A lunar eclipse occurs when Earth moves between the sun and the moon. Earth blocks some sunlight from reaching the moon, so the moon appears dark from Earth's shadow. A solar eclipse occurs when the moon moves between Earth and the sun. The moon blocks some sunlight from reaching Earth, so the sky grows dark. It is safe to view a lunar eclipse, but you should never look directly at a solar eclipse, even through sunglasses. Instead, make a pinhole projector. Cut a small square in the middle of a piece of cardboard. Place a piece of aluminum foil across it, and then poke a small hole in it so that the sun's light will shine onto another piece of cardboard. You can safely look at the sun's image on the second piece of cardboard.

1. What is the main idea of this story?
    a. You should never look directly at the sun.
    b. An eclipse happens when sunlight is blocked by Earth or the moon.
    c. The sky grows dark during a solar eclipse.

2. When does a lunar eclipse occur?

    _____

    _____

3. What does the moon look like during a lunar eclipse?

    _____

4. When does a solar eclipse occur?

    _____

    _____

5. How can you safely look at a solar eclipse?

    _____

Name _____

Read the story. Then, answer the questions.

Human-Made Satellites

A satellite is an object that orbits around another object. The moon is a natural satellite of Earth. There are also many human-made satellites orbiting Earth. People use satellites to communicate, track the weather, gather environmental data, plot accurate global positions, and conduct research. The first satellite, called *Sputnik*, was launched by Russia in 1957. *Sputnik* sent signals back to Earth for 22 days, until its transmitter ran out of power. The first U.S. satellite, called *Explorer*, was sent into space in 1958. Satellites can be launched either with a rocket or with the space shuttle. Today, over 2,000 satellites are orbiting Earth. Some people think there are too many satellites in space. It is very costly to bring them back to Earth, so when they stop working, they usually stay in orbit. If their orbit is very low, they may reenter Earth's atmosphere and burn up.

1. What is the main idea of this story?
   a. The first satellite was launched in 1957.
   b. Some people think there are too many satellites in space.
   c. Satellites orbit around other objects and can be natural or human-made.

2. What is a natural satellite of Earth?

   _____

3. What do people use satellites for?

   _____

   _____

   _____

4. When was the first U.S. satellite sent into space?

   _____

5. How are satellites launched?

   _____

Read the story. Then, answer the questions.

Primary and Secondary Sources

When you conduct research for a paper, you use sources. A primary source may be a letter, a diary, an interview, a speech, or a law. Primary sources provide firsthand information about an event from the view of someone who was writing when the event occurred. A secondary source may be an encyclopedia or a textbook, which collect and interpret information from other sources after an event has happened. If you look at the last page in an encyclopedia entry, you may see a list of articles and books that the author has consulted. A letter written home from a soldier serving in World War II is a primary source. It might tell about his experiences with other soldiers in a foreign country. A book that examines the role of the United States during World War II is a secondary source. It might discuss several soldiers' letters and draw conclusions from them.

1. What is the main idea of this story?
   a. A textbook is a secondary source.
   b. Primary sources are written by someone present at an event.
   c. Research includes the use of both primary and secondary sources.

2. What kind of information do primary sources provide?

   _____

3. What does a secondary source do?

   _____

   _____

4. What might an encyclopedia entry include on its last page?

   _____

   _____

5. Give an example of a primary source you might use to write a paper about the Klondike Gold Rush.

   _____

Read the story. Then, answer the questions.

The Canadian Prime Minister

The Canadian prime minister leads Canada's federal government. Although the prime minister is head of the government, the British monarch is head of the country. Before being elected, the prime minister must first become the leader of his or her political party. The leader of the party that wins the most seats in Parliament, the legislative body of the federal government, becomes the prime minister. Most of the prime ministers of Canada have been lawyers, but some have been business leaders, teachers, and doctors. The prime minister chooses a cabinet of advisors to help make important policy decisions. Leaders of the provinces, called premiers, often meet with the prime minister to discuss what is best for the people living in the provinces. The prime minister must also work with leaders from other countries to discuss issues that affect Canada and the world.

1. What is the main idea of this story?
   a. The Canadian prime minister leads the federal government.
   b. Some prime ministers work in other careers prior to being elected.
   c. The prime minister must sometimes meet with foreign leaders.

2. What is the role of the British monarch in the Canadian government?

   _____

3. How is the prime minister elected?

   _____

   _____

   _____

4. What are some jobs that prime ministers have held before being elected?

   _____

   _____

5. What role does the cabinet play in the government?

   _____

Name _____

Read the story. Then, answer the questions.

U.S. Presidential Elections

The people of the United States choose a new president every four years. This election takes place on the first Tuesday after the first Monday in November. Presidential candidates must be at least 35 years old and be native U.S. citizens. Before the general election in November, people in different U.S. states hold elections to determine each party's candidates. These state-level party elections are called primaries and caucuses. A primary is a lot like a regular election because people go to the polls to vote. At a caucus, people meet to discuss the candidates and then nominate the one they choose. After the state-level elections, the political parties hold national conventions to nominate and confirm their candidates. Each presidential candidate chooses a running mate for vice president and then begins campaigning around the country. After the election, the new president is sworn into office on January 20 of the next year.

1. What is the main idea of this story?
    a. Candidates campaign to be president for many months.
    b. The U.S. president is chosen through a series of state and national elections.
    c. A vice president must serve if something happens to the president.

2. What are the requirements to become the U.S. president?

    _____

    _____

3. What happens during a state primary?

    _____

4. What happens during a state caucus?

    _____

    _____

5. What happens at a national convention?

    _____

    _____

Read the story. Then, answer the questions.

Languages of Canada

Canada has two official languages: English and French. Because the Constitution lists these languages as official, all federal laws must be printed in both languages. Many other languages are also spoken in Canada, including Chinese, Spanish, and Arabic. There are also over 50 Aboriginal languages, or languages spoken by natives. One or two languages are more common in different provinces or geographical regions. In some more populous provinces, such as Ontario and British Columbia, a greater variety of languages are spoken. This may be because more immigrants from other countries live in these areas and bring their native languages to Canada. Each province may choose whether to designate an official provincial language. The official language of Quebec is French. It is the primary language for over 80 percent of the people who live there. A majority of the people in the province of Nunavut speak an Inuit language.

1. What is the main idea of this story?
    a. Most people in Canada speak either English or French.
    b. Over 50 Aboriginal languages are spoken in Canada.
    c. Canada has two official languages, but many others are also spoken in Canada.

2. Why must all Canadian federal laws be printed in both English and French?

    _____

    _____

3. What are Aboriginal languages?
    a. languages spoken by native peoples
    b. languages spoken only in Nunavut
    c. languages that are not written down

4. Why might more languages be spoken in some provinces than in others?

    _____

    _____

5. What is the official provincial language in Quebec?

    _____

Read the story. Then, answer the questions.

Languages of the United States

Although most people in the United States speak English, the country does not have an official language. English is used for official documents, laws, and court decisions. However, some areas require publications to be printed in another language if there are many speakers of that language living there. Thirty states have adopted English as their official language. Only one state, Hawaii, is officially bilingual. This means that the state recognizes two official languages, English and Hawaiian. Many people in the U.S. states bordering Mexico speak both English and Spanish. Other states, such as Louisiana and Maine, have a large number of French speakers. Many Native American languages are spoken on reservations, areas of land managed by native groups such as the Navajo and the Seminole. Because the United States is a nation of many immigrants, some people are reluctant to declare only one official language.

1. What is the main idea of this story?
   a. The United States has no official language, but many languages are spoken in the United States.
   b. Most people in the United States speak English.
   c. Spanish and French are spoken in some U.S. states.

2. What are some official publications for which English is used?

   _____

3. When might a publication need to be printed in another language?

   _____

   _____

4. Which two states have a large number of French speakers?

   _____

   _____

5. What is a reservation?

   _____

   _____

Read the story. Then, answer the questions.

Becoming a Canadian Citizen

Until 1947, people living in Canada were considered citizens of Great Britain. That year, the Canadian government passed a Citizenship Act declaring that its people were Canadian citizens. For the first time, they were able to use Canadian passports rather than British passports. Today, about 150,000 people become Canadian citizens every year. First, they must become permanent residents. This is a special legal status that says that a person has been approved to live permanently in Canada. After three years, a permanent resident is eligible to apply for Canadian citizenship. The person must be able to speak either English or French and must not have committed a crime in the past three years. The person must also pass a citizenship test to show that he or she knows Canadian history, geography, and government. After passing the test, new citizens take an oath during a citizenship ceremony declaring their allegiance to the British monarch and to Canada.

1. What is the main idea of this story?
    a. Canadians used to be British citizens.
    b. Many immigrants move to Canada each year.
    c. People who want to become Canadian citizens must complete several steps.

2. What did the Citizenship Act of 1947 declare?

    _____

    _____

3. How many people become Canadian citizens each year?

    _____

4. What does it mean to become a permanent resident of Canada?

    _____

    _____

5. What do citizens state when taking the oath of citizenship?

    _____

Name _____

Read the story. Then, answer the questions.

Becoming a U.S. Citizen

The United States is sometimes called a melting pot because its people come from many different countries and cultures. People who are born in the United States or who are born to U.S. citizens living outside the country are automatically U.S. citizens. People born elsewhere who want to become citizens must live in the United States for a certain amount of time and pass a citizenship test. This process is called naturalization. Each year, more than 450,000 people become U.S. citizens. To become a citizen, a person must have lived in the United States legally for at least five years and be able to read, write, and understand English. He or she must also pass a test covering the government, history, and Constitution of the United States. After meeting the other requirements, a new citizen must take an oath of allegiance to the United States in a special ceremony.

1. What is the main idea of this story?
   a. People who want to become U.S. citizens must meet certain requirements.
   b. Most U.S. citizens' families originally came from other countries.
   c. Many people move to the United States every year.

2. Why is the United States sometimes called a melting pot?

   _____

   _____

3. Which people are automatically U.S. citizens?

   _____

   _____

4. How many people become U.S. citizens each year?

   _____

5. What are two requirements to become a U.S. citizen?

   _____

   _____

   _____

Read the story. Then, answer the questions.

International Women's Day

International Women's Day is held on March 8. The first International Women's Day was celebrated in several European countries in 1911. The holiday was originally intended to promote the right of women to vote, earn equal pay to men, and hold public office. Many labor groups in different countries held marches to show their support for safe working environments and better wages for women. Today, people celebrate women's achievements in these areas but recognize that there is still a lot of work to do. In some countries, the holiday is similar to Mother's Day, and women receive gifts and bouquets of flowers from their families. In other countries, communities hold parades, political rallies, leadership development sessions, and career workshops for women. The United States designates the month of March as Women's History Month. Canada celebrates International Women's Week, a week of activities in March that honor women.

1. What is the main idea of this story?
   a. Some groups work to promote equal rights for women.
   b. International Women's Day recognizes achievements by women.
   c. The first International Women's Day was held in 1911.

2. When is International Women's Day held?

   _____

3. How is International Women's Day similar to Mother's Day?

   _____

   _____

4. What types of activities are held in some countries?

   _____

   _____

5. How does Canada honor women?

   _____

CD-104308 • © Carson-Dellosa

Name _____

Read the story. Then, answer the questions.

Labor Day

    Labor Day is a U.S. holiday celebrated on the first Monday in September. This day honors the achievements of U.S. workers. Labor Day was first celebrated in 1882 in New York City, New York, when the Central Labor Union held a public demonstration and a picnic. By 1894, over half of the U.S. states had adopted the holiday. Later that year, the U.S. Congress passed a law making Labor Day a federal holiday. Many communities hold parades on Labor Day to demonstrate the variety of different services that workers provide. Community leaders and government officials sometimes give speeches in support of workers' rights. Labor Day marks the end of summer because city swimming pools often close after this day, and many children return to school. People in Canada and the United States celebrate Labor Day on the same day, but many other countries celebrate International Workers' Day on May 1.

1. What is the main idea of this story?
   a. Many people hold parades on Labor Day.
   b. Labor Day honors the achievements of workers.
   c. Sometimes families have picnics on Labor Day.

2. When is Labor Day celebrated?

   _____

3. What happened on the first Labor Day?

   _____

   _____

4. When was Labor Day made an official U.S. federal holiday?

   _____

5. Which people might give speeches on Labor Day?

   _____

Read the story. Then, answer the questions.

Rural Communities

Rural communities are areas where few people live and there are not many large buildings. Rural residents may live on farms or in small towns. Rural schools are often smaller than those found in cities. There may be only one high school instead of several. Students who attend rural schools probably know each other better because they share many classes with each other. People in rural communities may need to rely on people living near them when the weather is bad. They may also pool resources so that the whole community helps out when one family needs assistance. Many people in rural areas enjoy riding horses or taking long walks in the countryside. They also enjoy the nature that exists around them. Some urban residents like to visit rural areas to escape the hustle and bustle of the city.

1. What is the main idea of this story?
   a. Rural towns are often very small.
   b. Rural residents often enjoy being outside in nature.
   c. Rural areas have few people or buildings.

2. How are rural schools different from those found in cities?

   _____

   _____

3. What is one advantage to living in a rural area?

   _____

   _____

4. What activities might people in rural areas enjoy?

   _____

   _____

5. Why do some urban residents like to visit rural areas?

   _____

Name _____

Read the story. Then, answer the questions.

Urban Communities

People who live in cities live in urban communities. They may live in houses or in apartment buildings. Urban residents often have less space than people who live in the countryside. They may ride a bicycle or use public transportation instead of driving a car. Many cities have excellent bus, train, or subway systems. Urban schools may have several hundred students in each grade. They may also offer a greater number of activities, such as sports teams and special clubs, as well as classes to prepare students for college. Many cities have public areas like parks and swimming pools that their residents can enjoy together. They may also have community programs like children's afterschool activities or luncheons for elderly people. Cities require many government workers to run smoothly. In urban communities, people must learn to work together.

1. What is the main idea of this story?
    a. Urban communities have many people who share a small amount of space.
    b. People in cities sometimes do not have cars.
    c. Urban residents may enjoy a variety of activities.

2. How might people in urban communities get to work or school?

    _____

    _____

3. What are some urban schools like?

    _____

    _____

4. Which public areas might urban residents enjoy together?

    _____

5. What kinds of community programs might a city have?

    _____

    _____

Read the story. Then, answer the questions.

Demographics

Demographics are characteristics of human populations. The word *demographics* contains the root words *demo*, meaning "people," and *graph*, meaning "to write." Demographic data includes people's ages, occupations, educational levels, and income levels. Government officials can use this information to determine the makeup of a city or country's population, and whether there is a need for different services. If a city's officials learn that there are a great number of senior citizens, they may recommend building a retirement center. If they learn that many families with young children are moving into the area, they may recommend building additional schools. One way that countries collect demographic data is by taking a national census. In the United States, an official census of the population is taken every 10 years. In Canada, a national census is taken every five years. Both countries use demographics to examine trends in their populations.

1. What is the main idea of this story?
    a. Rural cities may have fewer residents than urban ones.
    b. Some cities have a large number of young people.
    c. Demographics includes different kinds of information about people's lives.

2. What root words does *demographics* contain?

    _____

3. What types of information might demographic data include?

    _____

    _____

4. How do countries collect demographic data?

    _____

5. How often are censuses taken in the United States and Canada?

    _____

    _____

Name _____

Read the story. Then, answer the questions.

Coins and Cultures

Coins often show symbols of the cultures that produced them. Some ancient Greek coins had pictures of lions, geese, owls, turtles, or horses. Ancient Roman coins often included pictures of family members of the emperor. Their faces were shown in profile, or facing to the side. Coins in the United States do not have images of living people. On one side, a coin usually shows a famous U.S. president, and on the other, it usually shows a government building such as the Lincoln Memorial. The Canadian dollar coin, called the loonie, has a picture of a bird called a loon, which lives in areas of Canada. Other Canadian coins, including the penny, nickel, dime, and quarter, have pictures of Queen Elizabeth, the ruler of Great Britain, on one side. The other side of each coin shows an important symbol of Canada, including the maple leaf, the beaver, and the caribou.

1. What is the main idea of this story?
    a. Coins show symbols of the culture that produced them.
    b. Some coins have images of people on them.
    c. The maple leaf is an important symbol of Canada.

2. What animals were shown on ancient Greek coins?

   _____

3. What did ancient Roman coins often show?

   _____

4. What do most Canadian coins show?

   _____

5. How are U.S. coins different from Canadian coins?

   _____

   _____

   _____

Name _____

The main idea of a paragraph tells what that paragraph is about. The other sentences in the paragraph give details that support the main idea. In the paragraph below, the sentences are out of order. Put the sentences in the correct order so that the paragraph makes sense. Begin with the sentence that states the main idea.

Writing a Paper

Finally, publish your paper.

Fourth, proofread your paper for errors in spelling and grammar.

First, think about what you would like to write.

Make some notes about what you will write.

This is the stage where you change any words or ideas so that your paper will make more sense.

Third, make your paper better by revising it.

Share your finished paper with your friends and family.

Second, write a rough draft.

A draft is an early version of your paper that helps you develop your ideas.

There are five steps to writing a paper.

_____

_____

_____

_____

_____

_____

_____

_____

_____

_____

_____

 CD-104308 • © Carson-Dellosa

The main idea of a paragraph tells what that paragraph is about. The other sentences in the paragraph give details that support the main idea. In the paragraph below, the sentences are out of order. Put the sentences in the correct order so that the paragraph makes sense. Begin with the sentence that states the main idea.

Making a Fruit Salad

Fourth, chill the fruit salad in the refrigerator until you are ready to eat it.

You might choose oranges, bananas, apples, and strawberries.

First, buy some fruit at a store.

The fruit should be cut into bite-sized pieces.

You can also buy yogurt to mix with the fruit.

Third, put the fruit pieces into a large bowl.

Second, ask an adult to help you cut the fruit.

Stir the yogurt into the fruit mixture.

Finally, enjoy your tasty snack!

Fruit salad is an easy and tasty recipe that you can make for your family.

_____

_____

_____

_____

_____

_____

_____

_____

_____

_____

_____

_____

Name _____

The main idea of a paragraph tells what that paragraph is about. The other sentences in the paragraph give details that support the main idea. In the paragraph below, the sentences are out of order. Put the sentences in the correct order so that the paragraph makes sense. Begin with the sentence that states the main idea.

Writing a Letter

You should write a salutation, or greeting, under the heading.

Then, write a closing to your letter.

You should write the heading at the top of the page.

Finally, write your signature so that the person will know who the letter is from.

The salutation begins with "Dear" and includes the name of the person to whom you are writing.

A letter has several important parts.

The closing includes words like "sincerely" or "yours truly."

The body includes the information you want to tell the person.

A heading includes your address and the date.

Next, you should write the body of the letter.

_____

_____

_____

_____

_____

_____

_____

_____

_____

_____

_____

Name _____

The main idea of a paragraph tells what that paragraph is about. The other sentences in the paragraph give details that support the main idea. In the paragraph below, the sentences are out of order. Put the sentences in the correct order so that the paragraph makes sense. Begin with the sentence that states the main idea.

Solving a Problem

Finally, check your answer to see if your idea worked.

If not, go back to an earlier step and try a new way of solving the problem.

Breaking the problem-solving process into steps can make it easier.

This can help you make sure that you understand the problem.

Second, brainstorm ways you could solve the problem.

First, state the problem in your own words.

Compare your ideas with the ideas of your friends to determine which idea will work the best.

Sometimes a problem can seem difficult to solve.

Make a list of the pros and cons of each idea.

Third, choose one way to try to solve your problem.

_____

_____

_____

_____

_____

_____

_____

_____

_____

_____

_____

Name _____

The main idea of a paragraph tells what that paragraph is about. The other sentences in the paragraph give details that support the main idea. In the paragraph below, the sentences are out of order. Put the sentences in the correct order so that the paragraph makes sense. Begin with the sentence that states the main idea.

Writing a Book Report

First, choose a book to read.

Next, tell about the main character.

Finally, tell how the main character solved the problems.

While you are reading the book, take notes about the characters, setting, and plot.

Write the title of your book at the top of the page.

Writing a book report for a work of fiction can be easy if you break it into steps.

Start by describing the setting of the book.

At the end of your report, give your opinion of the book.

Then, write about the problems of the main character.

After you finish the book, you are ready to write your report.

_____

_____

_____

_____

_____

_____

_____

_____

_____

_____

_____

Missing Words

Read the story below. Every tenth word is missing. Fill in the blanks with the words from the word box below.

more	she	and	bike	broke
even	for	to	A	tighten
at	that	herself		

Lynne's friends had signed up for a bike race _____ the end of the summer. Lynne

had fixed her _____ many times, but she knew it was too old _____

worn for the race. Lynne walked with her brother _____ the bicycle shop. The owner,

Mrs. Perriman, was looking _____ someone to help fix bikes! Lynne told her how

_____ had helped her brother repair a flat tire and _____ the brakes

on his bike. She wanted to learn _____ about how bicycles were put together. Mrs.

Perriman said _____ she had a job for Lynne at the race. _____ good

mechanic was needed to help cyclists whose bicycles _____ down along the route.

Lynne thought that sounded like _____ more fun than riding a bike in the race

_____!

Missing Words

Read the story below. Every tenth word is missing. Fill in the blanks with the words from the word box below.

she	classmates	there	new	office
A	her	the	third	to
her	of	and		

Angelica was nervous about going to middle school. Her _____ from her old

school would make up only a _____ of the students in her grade. She knew that

_____ would be more classes to find in different parts _____ the

building. She would need to leave some of _____ books in her locker. Angelica's dad

took her to _____ middle school to enroll her in the right classes.

_____ friendly student named Kit smiled at her and offered _____

show her around. Kit showed Angelica the hall where _____ locker would be. Kit

walked Angelica to the cafeteria _____ the gym. When they got back to the school

_____, Angelica's dad was waiting for her. Angelica told him _____

was no longer nervous because she would have a _____ friend on the very first day.

Missing Words

Read the story below. Every eighth word is missing. Fill in the blanks with the words from the word box below.

grandfather	took	too	of	loves
Now	is	beach	learning	one
are	smell	was	visit	note
go	the			

Sharla and her family go to the _____ every summer to visit their grandfather. He _____ a fisherman. When Sharla was small, she _____ afraid to get in the water. She _____ swimming lessons and surprised her grandfather by _____ to swim before she visited him again. _____, Sharla's sister is learning to swim. Their _____ wants them to be safe when they _____ him. Everyone wears a life jacket in _____ boat. They check the weather before they _____ out on the ocean. They leave a _____ for Sharla's parents to tell where they _____ and when to expect them back. Sharla _____ to visit the beach. She likes the _____ of the saltwater and the golden shimmer _____ the sunlight on the water. She hopes _____ day she can live at the beach, _____.

Missing Words

Read the story below. Every eighth word is missing. Fill in the blanks with the words from the word box below.

play	said	the	with
music	similar	Aaron	the
There	director	called	could
times	the	which	choose

Aaron's aunt Sue played the clarinet in _____ orchestra. Aaron had seen her

perform many _____. Aunt Sue liked playing many kinds of _____,

from symphonies to jazz. Sometimes she played _____ a small group of only five

players, _____ a chamber quintet. Aaron wanted to join _____ school

band, but he was not sure _____ instrument he wanted to play. He liked

_____ clarinet, but he was not sure he _____ play it as well as Aunt

Sue. _____ were many other students who wanted to _____ the

clarinet, so Aaron thought he should _____ a different instrument to try. The band

_____ asked Aaron to try playing the saxophone. _____ loved the

sound it made! Aunt Sue _____ that the clarinet and saxophone are very

_____, so they could play duets together.

Missing Words

Read the story below. Every fifth word is missing. Fill in the blanks with the words from the word box below.

creating	difficult	runner	mom	She	Jena
find	first	mom	will	morning	able
Jena	with	raise	Jena	help	around
through	by	run	to	adult	the
she	aware				

Jena's mom is a _____. She competes in races _____ the United

States to _____ awareness of diabetes. Jena's _____ has diabetes

but is _____ to control its effects _____ medicine, diet, and

exercise. _____ rises early every morning _____ train for her

races _____ running up and down _____ hills around their house.

_____ often runs with her _____. She knows that by

_____ good habits today, she _____ be healthier as an

_____. At first it was _____ to wake up to _____

before dawn, but now _____ looks forward to it. _____ loves feeling

the cool _____ air and spending time _____ her mom. Next summer,

_____ will run in her _____ race. She wants to _____

her mom make others _____ of the need to _____ a cure for diabetes.

Compare and Contrast

When you describe the similarities between people, things, or events, you compare them. When you describe their differences, you contrast them.

Read the following stories and think about the comparisons and contrasts in each. Then, answer the questions below each story.

Amphibians and reptiles are both cold-blooded animals. Both live in many different areas of the world. Reptiles have hard-shelled eggs, but amphibians have soft, sticky eggs. When reptiles hatch, they look like tiny adults. Amphibians go through several life stages as they grow older.

What two things are being compared in this story?

_____

How are the two things similar? How are they different?

_____

_____

_____

_____

Books and newspapers are both things that people like to read. Books usually take more time to read because they are longer. Newspapers are published daily or weekly, while a book might be published only once. Newspapers tell about events in your community. Books tell about subjects that may be fictional, or made up by the author.

What two things are being compared in this story?

_____

How are the two things similar? How are they different?

_____

_____

_____

_____

 CD-104308 • © Carson-Dellosa

Compare and Contrast

When you describe the similarities between people, things, or events, you compare them. When you describe their differences, you contrast them.

Read the following stories and think about the comparisons and contrasts in each. Then, answer the questions below each story.

Storks and parakeets are both birds. Storks have very long legs and long necks. They do not sing. Storks wade into water to find fish to eat. In contrast, parakeets are sometimes kept as pets. They have short bills and can sing. They can even learn to talk if trained. They eat flowers, fruit, and seeds.

What two things are being compared in this story?

_____

How are the two things similar? How are they different?

_____

_____

_____

Aquariums and planetariums both have exhibits. An aquarium has animals such as fish and turtles that live in the water. A planetarium displays objects having to do with space, including pictures taken by astronauts and rocks brought back from the moon. Both museums can be good places to learn new things.

What two things are being compared in this story?

_____

How are the two things similar? How are they different?

_____

_____

_____

Compare and Contrast

When you describe the similarities between people, things, or events, you compare them. When you describe their differences, you contrast them.

Read the following stories and think about the comparisons and contrasts in each. Then, answer the questions below each story.

Biographies and mysteries are both types of books. A biography tells facts about a person's life. It might be written by that person or by someone else. A mystery is usually fictional, or made up. It describes how a puzzle or problem is solved by a detective, a police officer, or another person.

What two things are being compared in this story?

_____

How are the two things similar? How are they different?

_____

_____

_____

_____

Stars and planets are both objects in outer space. They are both very far from Earth and look like bright specks in the night sky. A planet is solid, but a star is a ball of hot gases. Planets get light from the sun, while stars produce their own light. Stars are extremely hot, but planets can be any temperature.

What two things are being compared in this story?

_____

How are the two things similar? How are they different?

_____

_____

_____

CD-104308 • © Carson-Dellosa

Name _____

Compare and Contrast

When you describe the similarities between people, things, or events, you compare them. When you describe their differences, you contrast them.

Read the following stories and think about the comparisons and contrasts in each. Then, answer the questions below each story.

Soccer and basketball are both sports played with a ball. Both are team sports that are played on a rectangular area. Soccer is played with the feet, while basketball is played with the hands. In soccer, the ball is kicked into a net, while in basketball, the ball is thrown through a hoop.

What two things are being compared in this story?

_____

How are the two things similar? How are they different?

_____

_____

_____

_____

Canada and the United States are both countries in North America. Canada is divided into provinces and territories, while the United States is divided into states. Canada is ruled by Parliament and the prime minister, while the United States has Congress and the president. Both countries have people who speak many different languages.

What two things are being compared in this story?

_____

How are the two things similar? How are they different?

_____

_____

_____

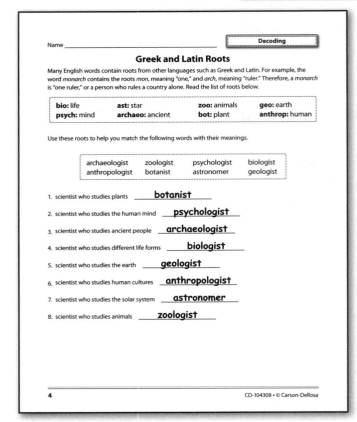

Name _____   **Decoding**

Greek and Latin Roots

Many English words contain roots from other languages such as Greek and Latin. For example, the word *monarch* contains the roots *mon*, meaning "one," and *arch*, meaning "ruler." Therefore, a *monarch* is "one ruler," or a person who rules a country alone. Read the list of roots below.

bio: life	**ast:** star	**zoo:** animals	**geo:** earth
psych: mind	**archaeo:** ancient	**bot:** plant	**anthrop:** human

Use these roots to help you match the following words with their meanings.

archaeologist	zoologist	psychologist	biologist
anthropologist	botanist	astronomer	geologist

1. scientist who studies plants   **botanist**
2. scientist who studies the human mind   **psychologist**
3. scientist who studies ancient people   **archaeologist**
4. scientist who studies different life forms   **biologist**
5. scientist who studies the earth   **geologist**
6. scientist who studies human cultures   **anthropologist**
7. scientist who studies the solar system   **astronomer**
8. scientist who studies animals   **zoologist**

4   CD-104308 • © Carson-Dellosa

Name _____   **Decoding**

Greek and Latin Roots

Many English words contain roots from other languages such as Greek and Latin. For example, the word *thermometer* contains the roots *therm* and *meter*. *Therm* means "heat," and *meter* means "to measure." Therefore, a *thermometer* is a device that measures heat. Read the list of roots below.

dent: tooth	**cardi:** heart	**neur:** nerve	**pod:** foot
hemo: blood	**ped:** child	**opt:** eye	**derm:** skin

Use these roots to match the following words with their meanings. Write the correct word in each blank.

cardiologist	hematologist	dermatologist	pediatrician
ophthalmologist	neurologist	podiatrist	dentist

1. doctor who examines blood   **hematologist**
2. doctor who examines feet   **podiatrist**
3. doctor who examines children   **pediatrician**
4. doctor who examines teeth   **dentist**
5. doctor who examines the nervous system   **neurologist**
6. doctor who examines skin   **dermatologist**
7. doctor who examines the heart   **cardiologist**
8. doctor who examines eyes   **ophthalmologist**

CD-104308 • © Carson-Dellosa   5

Name _____   **Decoding**

Greek and Latin Roots

Many English words contain roots from other languages such as Greek and Latin. For example, the word *semicircle* contains the roots *semi* and *circle*. *Semi* means "half," so a *semicircle* is half of a circle. Read the list of roots below.

mille: thousand	**poly:** many	**centi:** hundred	**quad:** four
tri: three	**hemi:** half	**equi:** equal	**oct:** eight

Use these roots to match the following words with their meanings. Write the correct word in each blank.

polygon	triangle	centimeter	hemisphere
octagon	quadrilateral	millisecond	equivalent

1. figure with many sides   **polygon**
2. having equal measure   **equivalent**
3. figure with three sides   **triangle**
4. half of a sphere   **hemisphere**
5. figure with four sides   **quadrilateral**
6. $\frac{1}{100}$ of a meter   **centimeter**
7. figure with eight sides   **octagon**
8. $\frac{1}{1,000}$ of a second   **millisecond**

6   CD-104308 • © Carson-Dellosa

Name _____   **Decoding**

Greek and Latin Roots

Many English words contain roots from other languages such as Greek and Latin. For example, the word *bicycle* contains the roots *bi* and *cycl*. *Bi* means "two," and *cycl* means "a circle or ring." Therefore, a *bicycle* is a vehicle that has two circles, or wheels. Read the list of roots below.

omni: all	**nutri:** nourish	**herba:** grass	**spir:** breathe
phys: body, nature	**carn:** meat	**aero:** air	**chlor:** green

Use these roots to help you match the following words with their meanings.

herbivore	nutrition	physical	respiration
aerobic	carnivore	chlorophyll	omnivore

1. something that makes plants' leaves green   **chlorophyll**
2. animal that eats only plants   **herbivore**
3. taking in the food necessary for health and growth   **nutrition**
4. the act of breathing   **respiration**
5. animal that eats only meat   **carnivore**
6. helping the body take in more oxygen   **aerobic**
7. relating to the body   **physical**
8. animal that eats all kinds of food   **omnivore**

CD-104308 • © Carson-Dellosa   7

Page 8

Name _____

Greek and Latin Roots

Many English words contain roots from other languages such as Greek and Latin. For example, the word *submarine* contains the roots *sub* and *marine*. *Sub* means "below," and *marine* means "water." Therefore, a *submarine* is a vehicle that travels below the water. Read the list of roots below.

ann: year	**auto:** self	**loc:** place	**chron:** time
dem: people	**fac:** make	**spec:** see	**biblio:** book

Use these roots to match the following words with their meanings.

democracy	bibliography	location	chronology
factory	spectator	anniversary	autobiography

1. place where things are made **factory**
2. position of something **location**
3. date marking a yearly event **anniversary**
4. person who watches something **spectator**
5. list of events in order **chronology**
6. book about a person's own life **autobiography**
7. government by the people **democracy**
8. list of reference books **bibliography**

8 CD-104308 • © Carson-Dellosa

Page 9

Name _____

Greek and Latin Roots

Many English words contain roots from other languages such as Greek and Latin. For example, the word *television* contains the roots *tele* and *vision*. *Tele* means "distance," and *vision* means "to see." Therefore, a *television* is an object that lets you see things from a distance. Read the list of roots below.

cred: believe	**jud:** law	**crypt:** hidden	**temp:** time
mar: sea	**leg:** read	**aud:** hear	**port:** carry

Use these roots to match the following words with their meanings.

audible	temporary	credible	marine
cryptic	judicial	legible	portable

1. able to be carried **portable**
2. relating to the law **judicial**
3. relating to the sea **marine**
4. able to be believed **credible**
5. lasting for only a short time **temporary**
6. able to be read **legible**
7. mysterious **cryptic**
8. able to be heard **audible**

CD-104308 • © Carson-Dellosa 9

Page 10

Name _____

Greek and Latin Roots

Many English words contain roots from other languages such as Greek and Latin. For example, the word *monorail* contains the roots *mono* and *rail*. *Mono* means "one," so a *monorail* is a vehicle that runs on a single rail. Read the list of roots below.

cap: take, seize	**brev:** short	**ver:** truth	**magn:** large
nomen: name	**alter:** other	**nov:** new	**cogn:** know

Use these roots to match the following words with their meanings.

alternate	recognize	abbreviate	magnify
novice	nominate	verify	captivate

1. to be familiar with **recognize**
2. to make larger **magnify**
3. to hold someone's attention **captivate**
4. to make shorter **abbreviate**
5. to change between two things **alternate**
6. to make sure something is true **verify**
7. to name someone as a candidate for office **nominate**
8. someone who is new at doing something **novice**

10 CD-104308 • © Carson-Dellosa

Page 11

Name _____

Greek and Latin Roots

Many English words contain roots from other languages such as Greek and Latin. For example, the word *international* contains the Latin root *inter*. *Inter* means "between," so something that is *international* happens between nations. Read the list of roots below.

mater: mother	**quer:** ask	**ped:** foot	**onym:** name
aqua: water	**frater:** brother	**arch:** leader	**pater:** father

Use these roots to match the following words with their meanings.

aquatic	monarch	paternal	pedometer
fraternal	query	antonym	maternal

1. motherly **maternal**
2. one ruler **monarch**
3. device that measures footsteps **pedometer**
4. brotherly **fraternal**
5. having to do with water **aquatic**
6. word that means the opposite **antonym**
7. question **query**
8. fatherly **paternal**

CD-104308 • © Carson-Dellosa 11

Worksheet 1 (page 12)

Name _____

Decoding

Compound Words

Compound words are two words that have been joined to form another word. They do not always keep the meanings of both words. For example, a *skyscraper* does not actually scrape the sky. A *skyscraper* is a very tall building. In the chart below, write the literal meaning for each word that makes up the compound word. Then, write what the compound word means. **Answers will vary.**

Compound Word	Literal Meaning for First Word	Literal Meaning for Second Word	Actual Meaning
1. airport	air: what you breathe	port: place for ships to dock	place where planes land
2. jellyfish	jelly: sweet spread for bread	fish: animal that swims	type of sea creature
3. newspaper	news: current events	paper: thin material made from pressed wood	printed paper with current events
4. upstairs	up: vertical direction	stairs: steps	on the floor above
5. playground	play: have fun	ground: earth	place where children play
6. bookkeeper	book: something you read	keeper: one who keeps something	someone who keeps records for a business
7. waterfall	water: liquid that people and animals drink	fall: tumble down	water that flows over a cliff
8. birthday	birth: being born	day: 24 hours	day someone is born
9. popcorn	pop: burst	corn: vegetable	corn that has been popped
10. afternoon	after: later than	noon: 12 o'clock	after 12 o'clock

12   CD-104308 • © Carson-Dellosa

Worksheet 2 (page 13)

Name _____

Decoding

Compound Words

Compound words are two words that have been joined to form another word. They do not always keep the meanings of both words. For example, a *turtleneck* sweater is not actually worn over the neck of a turtle. A *turtleneck* sweater is a sweater that covers your neck all the way to your chin. In the chart below, write the literal meaning for each word that makes up the compound word. Then, write what the compound word means. **Answers will vary.**

Compound Word	Literal Meaning for First Word	Literal Meaning for Second Word	Actual Meaning
1. tiptoe	tip: top of something	toe: part of the foot	walk very quietly
2. blueprint	blue: color	print: write letters	design that an architect uses
3. bedspread	bed: something people sleep on	spread: cover	covering for a bed
4. rainbow	rain: water that falls from the sky	bow: ribbon tied into a knot	an arc formed in the sky with colors
5. quicksand	quick: fast	sand: soft ground	sand that something can sink into
6. shoelace	shoe: something people wear on their foot	lace: a string that can be tied	tie for shoes
7. backyard	back: behind	yard: area of ground	area of ground behind the house
8. suitcase	suit: items of matched clothing	case: container	container to carry clothes in
9. cattail	cat: animal	tail: part of animal	type of reedy plant
10. toothbrush	tooth: what people and animals chew with	brush: tool with bristles	a tool to brush teeth

CD-104308 • © Carson-Dellosa   13

Worksheet 3 (page 14)

Name _____

Decoding

Compound Words

Compound words are two words that have been joined to form another word. They do not always keep the meanings of both words. For example, a *brainstorm* does not actually mean "a storm occurring in the brain." A *brainstorm* is when you think of a lot of ideas for solving a problem. In the chart below, write the literal meaning for each word that makes up the compound word. Then, write what the compound word means. **Answers will vary.**

Compound Word	Literal Meaning for First Word	Literal Meaning for Second Word	Actual Meaning
1. uproot	up: vertical direction	root: part of a plant	to pull up something
2. airplane	air: what something can breathe	plane: flat surface	something that people fly in
3. whirlpool	whirl: spin	pool: body of water	place where water spins downward
4. shortstop	short: not tall	stop: halt	baseball player
5. haircut	hair: something that grows on your head	cut: clip	to get hair clipped
6. clothespin	clothes: something to wear	pin: something that holds things together	pin that holds clothes on a line
7. postcard	post: mail	card: sturdy paper	card you send in the mail
8. supermarket	super: great or large	market: grocery store	large grocery store
9. teacup	tea: something to drink	cup: container	container used to drink tea
10. sailboat	sail: a piece of fabric	boat: small ship	small ship with a sail

14   CD-104308 • © Carson-Dellosa

Worksheet 4 (page 15)

Name _____

Decoding

Compound Words

Compound words are two words that have been joined to form another word. They do not always keep the meanings of both words. For example, an *anchorperson* is not a person who carries an anchor. An *anchorperson* is a person who reads news stories and introduces other news reporters on television. In the chart below, write the literal meaning for each word that makes up the compound word. Then, write what the compound word means. **Answers will vary.**

Compound Word	Literal Meaning for First Word	Literal Meaning for Second Word	Actual Meaning
1. buttercup	butter: spread made from milk	cup: container	type of flower
2. underground	under: below	ground: earth	below the earth
3. sandpaper	sand: soft dirt	paper: thin material made from pressed wood	rough paper used to make things smooth
4. downtown	down: opposite of up	town: city	area of city with many buildings or offices
5. fireplace	fire: flames	place: location	place to build a fire
6. pancake	pan: cooking utensil	cake: sweet baked food	thin cake cooked in a pan
7. sidewalk	side: edge	walk: move using legs	area to walk on next to the street
8. carpool	car: automobile	pool: small body of water	group of people who ride together in one car
9. grasshopper	grass: plant	hopper: something that hops	type of insect
10. haystack	hay: dried grass	stack: pile	pile of dried grass

CD-104308 • © Carson-Dellosa   15

Worksheet page 16

Name _____

Decoding

Compound Words

Compound words are two words that have been joined to form another word. They do not always keep the meanings of both words. For example, *frostbite* does not actually mean "being bitten by the frost." When you have *frostbite*, part of your body feels frozen from cold weather. In the chart below, write the literal meaning for each word that makes up the compound word. Then, write what the compound word means.

Answers will vary.

Compound Word	Literal Meaning for First Word	Literal Meaning for Second Word	Actual Meaning
1. paperback	paper: thin material made from pressed wood	back: reverse of something	book with a soft spine
2. earthquake	earth: ground	quake: shake	event in which the ground shakes
3. football	foot: body part at the end of the leg	ball: round object	game played with a ball
4. lighthouse	light: brightness	house: place where people live	building that provides light for ships
5. thumbprint	thumb: part of the hand	print: make an impression with ink	impression made with the thumb
6. necklace	neck: part of the body below the head	lace: something that can be tied	jewelry worn around the neck
7. bookcase	book: something you read	case: container	furniture that holds books
8. storeroom	store: supplies	room: area	area where supplies are kept
9. breakfast	break: split	fast: period of not eating	meal eaten in the morning
10. boxcar	box: container	car: automobile	part of a train

16

CD-104308 • © Carson-Dellosa

Worksheet page 17

Name _____

Decoding

Compound Words

Compound words are two words that have been joined to form another word. They do not always keep the meanings of both words. For example, something that is *offbeat* is not actually off the beat. Something that is *offbeat* is unusual or out of the ordinary. In the chart below, write the literal meaning for each word that makes up the compound word. Then, write what the compound word means.

Compound Word	Literal Meaning for First Word	Literal Meaning for Second Word	Actual Meaning
1. grandmother	grand: wonderful	mother: female parent	mother of a person's parent
2. paintbrush	paint: liquid used to cover walls	brush: tool with bristles	brush to paint with
3. software	soft: not hard	ware: something that is sold	computer program
4. partnership	partner: person that someone is paired with	ship: boat	working with someone
5. earring	ear: part of the head that someone can hear with	ring: metal circle	ring worn in the ear
6. scarecrow	scare: frighten	crow: type of bird	figure that frightens crows away
7. sunshine	sun: star that the planets orbit	shine: focus light on	light from the sun
8. armchair	arm: part of the body	chair: something to sit in	chair on which arms can be rested
9. overcoat	over: above	coat: jacket	coat worn over clothes
10. strawberry	straw: dried grass	berry: small circular fruit	type of fruit

Answers will vary.

CD-104308 • © Carson-Dellosa

17

Worksheet page 18

Name _____

Decoding

Shortened Words

Some words are shortened forms of longer words. For example, the word *ad* is short for *advertisement*. Read the sentences below. Fill in each blank with a word that is a shortened form of a word in the word box.

mathematics	airplane	telephone	refrigerator	veterinarian
influenza	gymnasium	teenager	draperies	examination

1. We put our leftovers in the **fridge** when we got home from the restaurant.

2. My stepdad took our dog to the **vet** because he needed a vaccination.

3. Lauri flew in a **plane** to her granddad's house in another state.

4. Every year, my mom gets a shot to make sure she does not get the **flu**.

5. Our basketball team practices after school in the **gym**.

6. Last night, I completed five pages in my **math** book.

7. My sister just turned 13, so she is a **teen** now.

8. Marisa said that she needed to make a **phone** call.

9. Next week, we have an **exam** in science class.

10. Grandma wants to put up new **drapes** in her living room.

18

CD-104308 • © Carson-Dellosa

Worksheet page 19

Name _____

Decoding

Shortened Words

Some words are shortened forms of longer words. For example, the word *wig* is short for *periwig*, a word that is no longer used by most people. Read the sentences below. Fill in each blank with a word that is a shortened form of a word in the word box.

luncheon	omnibus	necktie	automobile	champion
gasoline	memorandum	tuxedo	taxicab	popular

1. Some songs are part of **pop** culture.

2. My uncle took a **taxi** to the airport so that he could leave his car at home.

3. Theo is the **champ** on his soccer team.

4. We will eat **lunch** at noon.

5. The groom wore a **tux** to his wedding.

6. I ride the **bus** to and from school.

7. The principal sent out a **memo** to all of the teachers.

8. Dad wears a **tie** with a nice shirt when he goes to work.

9. Sylvie's mom stopped at the **gas** station on the way home.

10. Grandpa took his car to an **auto** mechanic.

CD-104308 • © Carson-Dellosa

19

Shortened Words

Some words are shortened forms of longer words. For example, the word *mart* is short for *supermarket*. Read the sentences below. Fill in each blank with a word that is a shortened form of a word in the word box.

dormitory	saxophone	bicycle	rhinoceros	graduate
laboratory	representative	limousine	photograph	submarine

1. Mom took a ___**photo**___ of my brother and me on our first day of school.
2. Lan plays the ___**sax**___ in the school band.
3. Manuel wants to be our class's ___**rep**___ on the student council.
4. The ___**rhino**___ has a large horn.
5. My cousin is now a college ___**grad**___.
6. Pamela rides her ___**bike**___ to school.
7. A ___**sub**___ takes people deep below the ocean's surface.
8. Susie's older brother lives in a college ___**dorm**___.
9. A scientist often works in the ___**lab**___.
10. My older sister and her friends took a ___**limo**___ to their school dance.

Shortened Words

Some words are shortened forms of longer words. For example, the word *clerk* is short for *cleric*, a word that is no longer used by most people. Read the sentences below. Fill in each blank with a word that is a shortened form of a word in the word box.

chimpanzee	logogram	hamburger	gemstone	condominium
technical	videotapes	biography	carbohydrates	delicatessen

1. My cousins and I like to watch old ___**videos**___ of our parents' childhoods.
2. The ___**deli**___ near our house serves delicious sandwiches.
3. The company's ___**logo**___ has two blue stars inside a red circle.
4. When the computer would not work, Mom called for ___**tech**___ support.
5. Aunt Edna lives in a new ___**condo**___ downtown.
6. I enjoyed reading the ___**bio**___ of Queen Elizabeth.
7. Juan would like a ___**burger**___ with his fries.
8. We saw a ___**chimp**___ named Freddy in the old movie.
9. Protein and ___**carbs**___ are different kinds of food.
10. The ___**gem**___ in Greta's ring sparkled in the sunlight.

Portmanteau Words

Portmanteau words were made by combining two words. For example, the word *brunch* was made by combining *breakfast* and *lunch*. Make a new word by combining the words in each row to make a word in the word box. Then, write what the new word means.

camcorder	flare	moped	glimmer	motel	smog
motorcade	crunch	splatter	spork	fanzine	sitcom

1. flame + glare = ___**flare**___ meaning: **burning light that glows**
2. smoke + fog = ___**smog**___ meaning: **pollution**
3. motorcar + parade = ___**motorcade**___ meaning: **parade of cars**
4. crispy + munch = ___**crunch**___ meaning: **to make noise when eating**
5. motor + hotel = ___**motel**___ meaning: **place you can stay overnight**
6. spoon + fork = ___**spork**___ meaning: **spoon-like utensil with tines**
7. gleam + shimmer = ___**glimmer**___ meaning: **a flickering light**
8. splash + spatter = ___**splatter**___ meaning: **to scatter liquid**
9. camera + recorder = ___**camcorder**___ meaning: **recording camera**
10. fan + magazine = ___**fanzine**___ meaning: **magazine devoted to a celebrity**
11. motor + pedal = ___**moped**___ meaning: **vehicle with pedals and a motor**
12. situation + comedy = ___**sitcom**___ meaning: **comedy TV show**

Answers will vary.

Synonyms

Synonyms are words that have nearly the same meaning. Read the sentences below. Choose the word in the word box that is a synonym for the boldfaced word. Then, write it on the line below the sentence.

considered	told	increase	threatened	critical
document	billfold	collecting	empty	

1. The storyteller **narrated** the tale in a deep, booming voice.
   ___**told**___

2. I received a **certificate** that said I had successfully completed the course.
   ___**document**___

3. The mayor said that providing funding for the hospital was an **urgent** issue.
   ___**critical**___

4. The judge **contemplated** the evidence before making her decision.
   ___**considered**___

5. That house has been **vacant** for several months.
   ___**empty**___

6. Dad took a $10 bill out of his **wallet** and handed it to the clerk.
   ___**billfold**___

7. The habitat of many animals is **endangered**.
   ___**threatened**___

8. My uncle has been **accumulating** baseball cards since he was a child.
   ___**collecting**___

9. The large speakers **amplify** the volume of the music.
   ___**increase**___

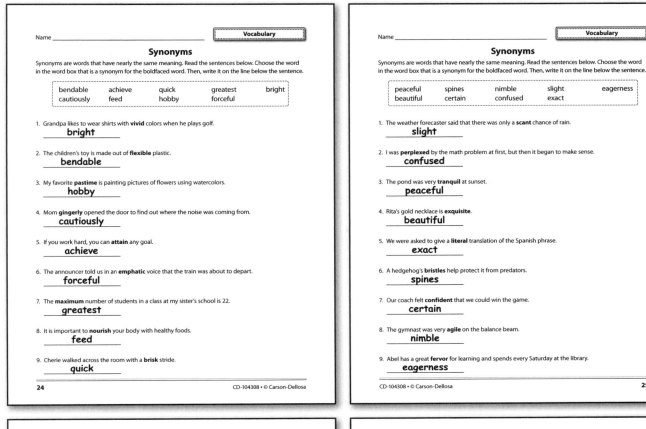

Name _____

Vocabulary

Synonyms

Synonyms are words that have nearly the same meaning. Read the sentences below. Choose the word in the word box that is a synonym for the boldfaced word. Then, write it on the line below the sentence.

bendable	achieve	quick	greatest	bright
cautiously	feed	hobby	forceful	

1. Grandpa likes to wear shirts with **vivid** colors when he plays golf.
   bright

2. The children's toy is made out of **flexible** plastic.
   bendable

3. My favorite **pastime** is painting pictures of flowers using watercolors.
   hobby

4. Mom **gingerly** opened the door to find out where the noise was coming from.
   cautiously

5. If you work hard, you can **attain** any goal.
   achieve

6. The announcer told us in an **emphatic** voice that the train was about to depart.
   forceful

7. The **maximum** number of students in a class at my sister's school is 22.
   greatest

8. It is important to **nourish** your body with healthy foods.
   feed

9. Cherie walked across the room with a **brisk** stride.
   quick

24   CD-104308 • © Carson-Dellosa

Name _____

Vocabulary

Synonyms

Synonyms are words that have nearly the same meaning. Read the sentences below. Choose the word in the word box that is a synonym for the boldfaced word. Then, write it on the line below the sentence.

peaceful	spines	nimble	slight	eagerness
beautiful	certain	confused	exact	

1. The weather forecaster said that there was only a **scant** chance of rain.
   slight

2. I was **perplexed** by the math problem at first, but then it began to make sense.
   confused

3. The pond was very **tranquil** at sunset.
   peaceful

4. Rita's gold necklace is **exquisite**.
   beautiful

5. We were asked to give a **literal** translation of the Spanish phrase.
   exact

6. A hedgehog's **bristles** help protect it from predators.
   spines

7. Our coach felt **confident** that we could win the game.
   certain

8. The gymnast was very **agile** on the balance beam.
   nimble

9. Abel has a great **fervor** for learning and spends every Saturday at the library.
   eagerness

CD-104308 • © Carson-Dellosa   25

Name _____

Vocabulary

Synonyms

Synonyms are words that have nearly the same meaning. Read the sentences below. Choose the word in the word box that is a synonym for the boldfaced word. Then, write it on the line below the sentence.

well-known	ridiculous	isolated	weak	struggled
imitate	external	objective	confirmed	

1. Ted felt **frail** after his illness last winter.
   weak

2. My **intention** is to finish my homework before dinner.
   objective

3. The **outward** appearance of the library may look old, but there are many new books inside.
   external

4. Marita wore an **absurd** costume in the play.
   ridiculous

5. The teacher **certified** that the grades were correct.
   confirmed

6. Frieda's uncle lives in a **secluded** house in the country.
   isolated

7. Dad **grappled** with the shutters before he finally closed them.
   struggled

8. Professor Wu is an **eminent** scholar.
   well-known

9. My little brother likes to **mimic** a cat when we are playing.
   imitate

26   CD-104308 • © Carson-Dellosa

Name _____

Vocabulary

Synonyms

Synonyms are words that have nearly the same meaning. Read the sentences below. Choose the word in the word box that is a synonym for the boldfaced word or phrase. Then, write it on the line below the sentence.

admiration	occupied	occupation	jostle	description
pleasant	blanket	delicate	see	

1. Ginny is always **cordial** to visitors who come to her house.
   pleasant

2. My brother wants to pursue the **profession** of firefighting.
   occupation

3. The **caption** under the painting said that it was painted in 1752.
   description

4. We have great **awe** for her talent as a pianist.
   admiration

5. That antique vase is very **fragile**.
   delicate

6. Uncle Roy had to **push and shove** the door to get it to close tightly.
   jostle

7. The meadow near my house is **inhabited** by rabbits and mice.
   occupied

8. We could barely **perceive** our house through the fog.
   see

9. Aunt Cathy sewed a **quilt** from fabric scraps.
   blanket

CD-104308 • © Carson-Dellosa   27

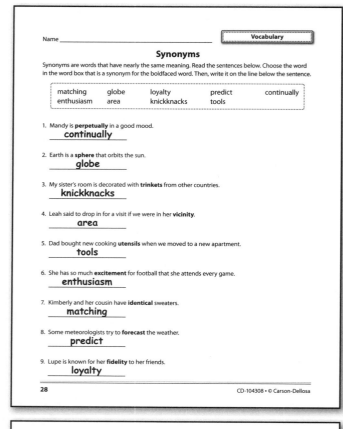

Page 28

Name _____ Vocabulary

Synonyms

Synonyms are words that have nearly the same meaning. Read the sentences below. Choose the word in the word box that is a synonym for the boldfaced word. Then, write it on the line below the sentence.

| matching | globe | loyalty | predict | continually |
| enthusiasm | area | knickknacks | tools | |

1. Mandy is **perpetually** in a good mood.
   continually

2. Earth is a **sphere** that orbits the sun.
   globe

3. My sister's room is decorated with **trinkets** from other countries.
   knickknacks

4. Leah said to drop in for a visit if we were in her **vicinity**.
   area

5. Dad bought new cooking **utensils** when we moved to a new apartment.
   tools

6. She has so much **excitement** for football that she attends every game.
   enthusiasm

7. Kimberly and her cousin have **identical** sweaters.
   matching

8. Some meteorologists try to **forecast** the weather.
   predict

9. Lupe is known for her **fidelity** to her friends.
   loyalty

28   CD-104308 • © Carson-Dellosa

Page 29

Name _____ Vocabulary

Synonyms

Synonyms are words that have nearly the same meaning. Read the sentences below. Choose the word in the word box that is a synonym for the boldfaced word. Then, write it on the line below the sentence.

| unbiased | products | previous | liquids | lift |
| chime | exciting | decorated | stylish | |

1. When you are ill, you should drink plenty of **fluids**.
   liquids

2. We paid for our **merchandise** and left the store.
   products

3. The bells **peal** every day at noon.
   chime

4. The referee gave us her **neutral** opinion about which team had scored the point.
   unbiased

5. Grandpa wears a **jaunty** hat when he goes to a parade.
   stylish

6. It took five people to **hoist** the couch into the truck.
   lift

7. We took an **exhilarating** ride on the roller coaster.
   exciting

8. Sometimes we receive mail for our home's **former** occupant.
   previous

9. The store window was **ornamented** with lights and ribbons.
   decorated

CD-104308 • © Carson-Dellosa   29

Page 30

Name _____ Vocabulary

Antonyms

Antonyms are words that have opposite meanings. Read the sentences below. Choose the word in the word box that is an antonym for the boldfaced word. Then, write it on the line below the sentence.

| slower | dull | afterword | maximum | absent |
| bought | different | before | depleted | |

1. The **minimum** charge for admission to the play is $3.
   maximum

2. My two brothers look very **similar**.
   different

3. Depending on the weather, I may be **present** for the hike tomorrow.
   absent

4. The dance team practices **after** school.
   before

5. The horse's gait grew **faster** when the rider gave it the command.
   slower

6. Grandma **sold** her house last year.
   bought

7. Mom wants to paint our living room in **vivid** colors.
   dull

8. The snack tray was **replenished** halfway through the party.
   depleted

9. The **foreword** told why the author wrote the book.
   afterword

30   CD-104308 • © Carson-Dellosa

Page 31

Name _____ Vocabulary

Antonyms

Antonyms are words that have opposite meanings. Read the sentences below. Choose the word in the word box that is an antonym for the boldfaced word. Then, write it on the line below the sentence.

| smooth | old | gloomy | depreciate | tranquil |
| final | simple | near | common | |

1. Gene's face was **radiant** after the game ended.
   gloomy

2. The salesperson asked whether we were looking for anything **special**.
   common

3. The cafeteria was very **hectic** at lunchtime.
   tranquil

4. Some animals have very **rough** fur.
   smooth

5. My brother can see objects that are **far** away with his new glasses.
   near

6. The coach's **initial** thought was that the team would win the game.
   final

7. The quilt in my room has an **elaborate** design on one side.
   simple

8. When you invest money, sometimes it will **appreciate**.
   depreciate

9. Many people are looking to use **new** sources of energy.
   old

CD-104308 • © Carson-Dellosa   31

Name _____

Antonyms

Antonyms are words that have opposite meanings. Read the sentences below. Choose the word in the word box that is an antonym for the boldfaced word. Then, write it on the line below the sentence.

young	lengthen	calm	found	urban
giant	excludes	rigid	unusual	

1. Some people **abbreviate** their names.

    lengthen

2. Our teacher said that the exam schedule was **flexible**.

    rigid

3. Nancy's little sister **lost** her ball.

    found

4. A **typical** Saturday activity for me is running in the park with my mom.

    unusual

5. Someday I would like to live in a **rural** area.

    urban

6. Our math homework **involves** fractions and decimals.

    excludes

7. The store was **lively** on the day before the holiday.

    calm

8. Uncle Vic baked **miniature** cupcakes for the bake sale.

    giant

9. I played the game with my **elderly** uncle.

    young

Name _____

Multiple Meanings

Many words have more than one meaning. The way a word is used in a sentence can help you figure out which meaning is being used. Read the sentences below. Choose the correct meaning of the boldfaced word or phrase as it is used in the sentence. Then, circle the letter of the correct meaning of the word or phrase.

1. The engineers were afraid that the bridge would **buckle** under too much weight.
    a. piece of metal worn in the middle of a belt
    (b.) collapse or give way under pressure

2. The committee will **deliberate** on the issues.
    (a.) discuss before making a decision
    b. done on purpose after careful consideration

3. Amie **chimed in** with her ideas for the bake sale.
    (a.) interrupted or added to the discussion
    b. rang to indicate the time

4. The mayor's popularity **soared** after her speech.
    a. flew high into the air
    (b.) rose sharply

5. Dad **pried** open the door to the shed.
    a. interfered with someone's personal business
    (b.) forced apart with a lever

6. Please **relay** my message to the principal.
    (a.) communicate or pass along to
    b. race with a team of runners

7. We **scoured** the park for the clues to the mystery.
    a. scrubbed clean
    (b.) searched thoroughly

8. A **plume** of smoke rose from the chimney.
    a. feather of a bird
    (b.) long column or band

Name _____

Multiple Meanings

Many words have more than one meaning. The way a word is used in a sentence can help you figure out which meaning is being used. Read the sentences below. Choose the correct meaning of the boldfaced word as it is used in the sentence. Then, circle the letter of the correct meaning of the word.

1. We tried to **prod** him into joining the team.
    (a.) urge someone on
    b. nudge or poke sharply

2. Deanna's **rash** decision caused her to lose the game.
    (a.) hasty or reckless
    b. skin inflammation

3. Mom paid a **toll** when we crossed the bridge.
    a. ring like a bell
    (b.) small tax or fee

4. Jared could not **fathom** how his team had won the game.
    a. depth of six feet (1.8 m)
    (b.) come to understand

5. Her **initial** reaction to the rain was to cancel the race.
    (a.) first or beginning
    b. capital letter of a name

6. Aunt Ceci will have surgery for a pinched **nerve**.
    (a.) part of the body
    b. courage or daring

7. The river has a very high **bank**.
    a. a place to keep money
    (b.) a slope or hill

8. We asked the cashier to **void** our transaction.
    (a.) cancel
    b. empty space

Name _____

Multiple Meanings

Many words have more than one meaning. The way a word is used in a sentence can help you figure out which meaning is being used. Read the sentences below. Choose the correct meaning of the boldfaced word as it is used in the sentence. Then, circle the letter of the correct meaning of the word.

1. The representative used her office as a **vehicle** for communicating her views.
    a. type of transportation
    (b.) means of expression

2. Mom will **cinch** the belt around her waist.
    (a.) fasten tightly
    b. something certain to happen

3. The farmer made **furrows** in the earth with the plow.
    (a.) deep troughs to plant crops in
    b. wrinkles in a person's brow

4. My teacher asked me to **condense** my report to one page.
    a. change from vapor to liquid water
    (b.) make shorter or more compact

5. Anthony's great-grandfather was a **distinguished** professor.
    a. told two things apart from each other
    (b.) be famous for accomplishments

6. I **skimmed** the material again before the test.
    (a.) looked at quickly
    b. glided across

7. We were asked to **refrain** from talking during the assembly.
    (a.) avoid
    b. repeated part of a song

8. The city's new development **sprawls** over many miles.
    a. lies down
    (b.) stretches out

Name _____   Vocabulary

Multiple Meanings

Many words have more than one meaning. The way a word is used in a sentence can help you figure out which meaning is being used. Read the sentences below. Choose the correct meaning of the boldfaced word as it is used in the sentence. Then, circle the letter of the correct meaning of the word.

1. To what **degree** do you agree with his remarks?
   a. measurement of temperature
   (b.) extent of a condition

2. I could not **contain** my enthusiasm about my new bicycle.
   a. enclose in a jar
   (b.) keep under control

3. The director **posted** the results from the audition for the play.
   a. a pole set up to mark something
   (b.) to announce publicly

4. My first **impression** of my new school was that I liked it very much.
   (a.) feeling
   b. imprint

5. The tapestry has **elaborate** designs on it.
   (a.) detailed or complex
   b. tell more about

6. The map has a **legend** to tell us what the symbols mean.
   a. story told from the past
   (b.) explanation of symbols

7. The science test was **tough**, but I think I did well.
   a. hard to chew
   (b.) difficult

8. I felt **sheer** relief when the swim meet was over.
   (a.) absolute
   b. transparent

CD-104308 • © Carson-Dellosa   36

Name _____   Vocabulary

Multiple Meanings

Many words have more than one meaning. The way a word is used in a sentence can help you figure out which meaning is being used. Read the sentences below. Choose the correct meaning of the boldfaced word as it is used in the sentence. Then, circle the letter of the correct meaning of the word.

1. The fisherman told a funny **yarn** about life at sea.
   a. thick thread used for knitting
   (b.) tale that is hard to believe

2. The bike shop charges a **flat** rate for replacing tires.
   (a.) set or not varying
   b. smooth and even

3. Last year, my father learned how to **operate** a computer.
   (a.) use the controls on
   b. perform surgery

4. The tree branch **grated** against the window.
   a. irritated
   (b.) scraped

5. Mom said that my new sunglasses **suit** me.
   (a.) look appropriate on
   b. matched set of clothing

6. Scientists say that Earth's **core** is very hot.
   a. set of basic classes
   (b.) innermost part

7. The candidate might **flounder** if someone asks about an unfamiliar issue.
   (a.) struggle for words
   b. type of fish

8. We are planning a trip to **scale** that mountain.
   (a.) climb or rise gradually
   b. device used for weighing

CD-104308 • © Carson-Dellosa   37

Name _____   Vocabulary

Multiple Meanings

Many words have more than one meaning. The way a word is used in a sentence can help you figure out which meaning is being used. Read the sentences below. Choose the correct meaning of the boldfaced word as it is used in the sentence. Then, circle the letter of the correct meaning of the word.

1. The U.S. president's **cabinet** must be approved by the Senate.
   a. wooden cupboard
   (b.) council of advisors

2. Grandma **grilled** vegetables for dinner.
   (a.) cooked over a fire
   b. questioned intensely

3. That antique painting has **appreciated** over time.
   (a.) increased in value
   b. felt grateful for

4. A good education is **critical** for success later in life.
   a. disapproving
   (b.) important

5. The banker deposited $500 in the **vault**.
   a. piece of gymnastic equipment
   (b.) large safe

6. We enjoyed the **sparkling** conversation at the party.
   a. glittering
   (b.) interesting

7. Reyna put the horse in the **stall** after she groomed him.
   (a.) area of a barn
   b. halt or pause

8. Matthew thought of a **novel** approach to solving the problem.
   (a.) new or innovative
   b. fictional book

CD-104308 • © Carson-Dellosa   38

Name _____   Vocabulary

Definitions

Read the sentences below. Use the context clues to figure out the definition of each boldfaced word. Then, write the letter of the correct definition on the line.

a. to show how   f. able to be changed
b. people who move from another country   g. provide nutrients
c. decision   h. usually
d. made shorter   i. mechanical device
e. plans   j. forecasted

1. The word *doctor* can be **abbreviated** as *Dr.* __d__
2. Ms. Yang **demonstrated** how to complete the experiment. __a__
3. My brother and I **typically** spend each summer at our grandmother's house. __h__
4. The sportscaster **predicted** that the visiting team would win the game. __j__
5. My **schedule** includes activities every day after school. __e__
6. The coach asked us to keep our plans **flexible** in case our team made the playoffs. __f__
7. Eating a variety of foods helps to **nourish** the body. __g__
8. My mother's parents were **immigrants** from Russia. __b__
9. Mom fixed the **mechanism** so that she could move the garage door up and down. __i__
10. The judge said that she had reached a **verdict**. __c__

CD-104308 • © Carson-Dellosa   39

Page 40

Name _____

Vocabulary

Definitions

Read the sentences below. Use the context clues to figure out the definition of each boldfaced word. Then, write the letter of the correct definition on the line.

a. a part played by an actor
b. at the edge
c. common saying
d. left out
e. characteristics of a surface

f. satisfied
g. at the same time
h. pull out
i. took back
j. stages

1. My uncle used a hammer to **wrench** the nail out of the board. __h__

2. Daniel tried out for a **role** in the school play. __a__

3. Silk has a very smooth **texture**. __e__

4. Our class called out the answer to the question in **unison**. __g__

5. I **retrieved** my hat from the lost-and-found box. __i__

6. We learned about the **phases** of the moon in science class. __j__

7. Tony **quenched** his thirst after the race by drinking water. __f__

8. The scientists believed that they were on the **verge** of finding a cure for the disease. __b__

9. An old **maxim** is "A stitch in time saves nine." __c__

10. The teacher accidentally **omitted** Cathy's name from the list. __d__

Page 41

Name _____

Vocabulary

Definitions

Read the sentences below. Use the context clues to figure out the definition of each boldfaced word. Then, write the letter of the correct definition on the line.

a. small fragment of something
b. first or at the beginning
c. area around and including a city
d. someone speaking
e. to inspire

f. small printed paper
g. feeling or guess
h. does well
i. put into action
j. speaks nonsense

1. My **initial** impression was that soccer was a difficult game, but I soon changed my mind. __b__

2. The **narrator** of the documentary spoke in a very soft voice. __d__

3. The volunteers passed out a **pamphlet** listing ways people could help clean up the environment. __f__

4. We will try to **implement** our new plan next week. __i__

5. I have a **hunch** that it will snow tomorrow. __g__

6. Mom is good at **motivating** me to do well in everything I try. __e__

7. She thought she had found the missing puzzle **piece**. __a__

8. Last year, we moved from a rural area to a **metropolitan** region. __c__

9. Candace **excels** at math and science. __h__

10. Joey's little sister is learning to talk, but right now she **babbles**. __j__

Page 42

Name _____

Vocabulary

Definitions

Read the sentences below. Use the context clues to figure out the definition of each boldfaced word. Then, write the letter of the correct definition on the line.

a. large meeting
b. calm or relaxed
c. school grounds
d. do well
e. to convince

f. live in
g. manner of speaking
h. brought together
i. large dish
j. liquid to drink

1. Laura spoke with a foreign **accent** as part of her character in a play. __g__

2. There was a guest speaker on **campus** last week. __c__

3. My favorite **beverage** is lemonade. __j__

4. My mom was out of town last month at a **convention**. __a__

5. Lydia is a **serene** person who never raises her voice. __b__

6. Please put the fruit slices on the serving **platter**. __i__

7. The sisters were **reconciled** after 10 years. __h__

8. Some plants **thrive** in rocky soil. __d__

9. A diverse range of people **inhabit** our town. __f__

10. We tried to **coax** Max into playing the fiddle for us. __e__

Page 43

Name _____

Vocabulary

Definitions

Read the sentences below. Use the context clues to figure out the definition of each boldfaced word. Then, write the letter of the correct definition on the line.

a. put forward
b. not well-known
c. manner of walking
d. wool
e. book about a person's life

f. pushed by bumping
g. in part
h. to begin or start
i. noticed
j. figured out

1. Our assignment is to write a summary of a **biography**. __e__

2. Mia **asserted** her opinion at the meeting. __a__

3. Please take your seats because the presentation is about to **commence**. __h__

4. We **deduced** the answer to the problem. __j__

5. The topic of her report is an **obscure** painter from the Middle Ages. __b__

6. My project is only **partially** complete. __g__

7. Amanda has a very fast **gait**, so it is hard to keep up with her. __c__

8. My arm was **jostled** when someone tried to move past me in the crowd. __f__

9. The science teacher asked us to write everything we **perceived**. __i__

10. The sheep's **fleece** was thick. __d__

Definitions (Page 44)

Read the sentences below. Use the context clues to figure out the definition of each boldfaced word. Then, write the letter of the correct definition on the line.

a. full of detail
b. hurried
c. the study of words
d. to take care of immediately
e. pledge of assurance
f. list of food options
g. to be careful with something
h. driving force
i. think ahead
j. makes wrinkles

1. In our language arts class, we are learning **grammar**. __c__
2. Dad **furrows** his brow when you ask him a tough question. __j__
3. The **menu** lists seven different sandwiches. __f__
4. Caleb drew an **intricate** design on the mural. __a__
5. The mayor says that the city must be **prudent** with its money. __g__
6. I like to **speculate** about what career might be in my future. __i__
7. Mom said that it is **urgent** that I clean my room because Granddad is coming to visit. __d__
8. The store offered a **guarantee** that it would fix any problems that occurred within the first 30 days after purchase. __e__
9. Our team had enough **momentum** after the first half to win the game. __h__
10. Aunt Faye **bustled** around getting ready to leave the house. __b__

Definitions (Page 45)

a. exactly like
b. leave out
c. a document written by hand
d. breakfast food made from grain
e. quieted down
f. shiny surface
g. someone who helps
h. introduction
i. breathtaking
j. thought about

1. The potter put a special **glaze** on her mugs and bowls. __f__
2. When I looked down at my shoes, I realized that my socks were not **identical**. __a__
3. The librarian showed us a rare **manuscript** from the fourteenth century. __c__
4. The view from the mountaintop was **exhilarating** after the long climb. __i__
5. My dad **pondered** my question for a long time before answering. __j__
6. The chatter **subsided** as the speaker walked onto the stage. __e__
7. Our reading club does not **exclude** anyone who loves to read. __b__
8. The author explained the book's purpose in its **preface**. __h__
9. Timothy is my best **ally** on the team; we work together well. __g__
10. I often eat a bowl of **cereal** before I go to school. __d__

Definitions (Page 46)

a. the same as
b. tradition
c. to be very different
d. deep thinking
e. handwritten names
f. at the edge or onset
g. abundant, luxurious
h. member of a profession
i. friends
j. to plan to do something

1. Due to decreased sales, the business is on the **brink** of bankruptcy. __f__
2. Our family **custom** is to go to Grandma's house for New Year's Eve. __b__
3. Erin and I have been best **pals** since first grade. __i__
4. One foot is **equivalent** to 12 inches. __a__
5. In the school play, I wore an **outlandish** hat with a giant flower. __c__
6. If it snows, someone on the school's **faculty** will contact the TV station about canceling school. __h__
7. Michaela **intends** to enroll in medical school after college. __j__
8. The club hung **lavish** decorations for the banquet. __g__
9. That book makes a **profound** statement about the world today. __d__
10. Some people have elaborate **signatures** with many swirls. __e__

Definitions (Page 47)

a. to ask questions
b. threw away
c. wonder
d. charming
e. type of poetry
f. dried
g. revealed in secret
h. conditions
i. restored confidence
j. made louder

1. Grandma **assured** me that I would perform better in the next game. __i__
2. I **queried** the teacher because I did not understand the project requirements. __a__
3. Shakespeare was known for his 14-line **sonnets**. __e__
4. We watched the professional basketball players and were in **awe** at their skill. __c__
5. It was not clear under what **circumstances** Dad would be needed at the office over the weekend. __h__
6. Amelia **discarded** her sandwich wrapper. __b__
7. I **raised** my voice so that everyone could hear my speech. __j__
8. Wendy **confided** that she would try out for the play. __g__
9. We brought **dehydrated** apricots for a snack. __f__
10. The old-fashioned movie was **enchanting**. __d__

Name _____

Definitions

Read the sentences below. Use the context clues to figure out the definition of each boldfaced word. Then, write the letter of the correct definition on the line.

a. handed out
b. watches over
c. group of sentences
d. an award
e. to remember

f. not able to be seen
g. to move quickly
h. native environment
i. went before
j. to copy or imitate

1. My brother **briskly** raked the leaves so that he could go to the movies with his friends. **g**

2. The employee received a **commendation** for her excellent service. **d**

3. The teacher **distributed** the worksheets for us to complete. **a**

4. A series of advertisements **preceded** the movie. **i**

5. In my **recollection**, last summer was a lot of fun. **e**

6. A lifeguard **supervises** swimmers at a beach. **b**

7. Sarita can **mimic** any voice she hears. **j**

8. An amphibian's **habitat** is part land and part water. **h**

9. Germs are **invisible** without a microscope. **f**

10. Your paper should begin with an introductory **paragraph**. **c**

48   CD-104308 • © Carson-Dellosa

Name _____

Read the story. Then, answer the questions.

Hammurabi's Code

One reason that modern countries run smoothly is that their laws are published. Because of this, all citizens know what laws they must follow. During ancient times, laws were not always recorded. A Babylonian king named Hammurabi created the first set of written laws for his people around 1760 B.C.E. He wanted to bring all of the people in his empire together under one set of laws. Because the laws were written down, everyone, whether rich or poor, was expected to obey them. Hammurabi's Code included 282 laws written in cuneiform, a type of writing in which symbols were carved into clay tablets. Each law included a penalty, or punishment, for disobeying it. The laws were written on a stela, which was a large slab of stone that was posted for all to see. Archaeologists working in the area now known as Iran discovered the stela in 1901. Spectators may view Hammurabi's Code in the Louvre Museum in Paris.

1. What is the main idea of this story?
   a. Modern countries publish their laws.
   b. Hammurabi's Code was an ancient set of laws.
   c. Archaeologists often find ancient materials.

2. Who was Hammurabi?
   an ancient Babylonian king who created the first set of written laws

3. Why did Hammurabi write down his laws?
   to bring all the people in his empire together under one set of laws

4. Where were Hammurabi's laws written?
   on a large slab of stone called a stela

5. Where did archaeologists find Hammurabi's Code?
   in what is now Iran

CD-104308 • © Carson-Dellosa   49

Name _____

Read the story. Then, answer the questions.

Athens and Sparta

Athens and Sparta were two important city-states in ancient Greece. A city-state is a region controlled by one city that is usually part of a larger cultural area. The citizens of both Athens and Sparta were ruled by elected assemblies. In addition, Athens had elected leaders called archons, while Sparta had kings who governed until they died or were overthrown. The people of Athens valued education and the arts and sciences. However, the people of Sparta focused on military life. Men in Sparta had to serve in the military from a young age, while men in Athens could choose whether to serve or not. The Greek city-states fought each other during the Peloponnesian War, from 431 to 404 B.C.E. Although Sparta defeated Athens, it was conquered later by the city of Thebes. Today, the city of Sparta is remembered for its military skill. In contrast, Athens is remembered for its philosophers and writers.

1. What is the main idea of this story?
   a. The city of Thebes was also located in Greece.
   b. Sparta's kings ruled until they died or were overthrown.
   c. Sparta and Athens were two very different city-states in ancient Greece.

2. What is a city-state?
   region controlled by a city that is part of a larger cultural area

3. How were the governments of ancient Athens and Sparta different?
   Sparta had kings, while Athens had elected leaders.

4. How were the governments of ancient Athens and Sparta similar?
   Both had elected assemblies that governed the people.

5. What is Athens remembered for today?
   its philosophers and writers

50   CD-104308 • © Carson-Dellosa

Name _____

Read the story. Then, answer the questions.

Alexander the Great

Alexander the Great was the son of a Macedonian king. He was born in 356 B.C.E. Alexander learned about Greek culture from his teachers, including the famous philosopher Aristotle. Alexander became king at age 20, when his father died. He spread the Greek culture to foreign areas covering over 22 million square miles (nearly 57 million square kilometers). Alexander was an unusual ruler because he allowed people in different areas to govern themselves as long as they followed Greek customs. Alexander's empire shared a common currency and language, and many cities were named Alexandria in his honor. People from different parts of the empire, such as the Middle East and India, began to share knowledge with each other. This led to great achievements in science and art. Alexander died at age 33, and his empire was split among three generals. Alexander's empire was later absorbed into the Roman Empire.

1. What is the main idea of this story?
   a. Alexander the Great was an important leader in ancient times.
   b. Alexander was the son of a Macedonian king.
   c. Aristotle was a great philosopher of ancient Greece.

2. How did Alexander learn about Greek culture?
   from his teachers

3. What made Alexander an unusual leader?
   He let people govern themselves if they followed Greek customs.

4. What similarities did parts of Alexander's empire share?
   common currency and language and many cities named Alexandria

5. What happened to Alexander's empire after his death?
   It was divided among three generals and was later absorbed into the Roman Empire.

CD-104308 • © Carson-Dellosa   51

Name _____

Read the story. Then, answer the questions.

The Tang Dynasty

For many years, China was governed by a series of dynasties, or rulers from the same family. The Tang Dynasty, which ruled from about 618 to 907 A.D., is considered China's Golden Age. Theater, dancing, sculpting, and painting were all very popular during this time. The capital city, Chang'an, had over one million people. Farmers were allowed to own land, although this later changed. People who wanted to work in the government had to pass a difficult exam. Only the smartest and most educated people could serve as government officials. The Tang government took a census to determine the empire's population, and households paid taxes on grain and cloth. Trade inside China and to other countries flourished because new roads and waterways made it easier to travel. Today, the Tang Dynasty is seen as a time of great cultural achievement.

1. What is the main idea of this story?
   a. The Tang government taxed grain and cloth.
   b. The Tang Dynasty lasted for nearly 300 years.
   (c.) The Tang Dynasty was a period of great cultural achievement.

2. What artistic activities were popular during the Tang Dynasty?
   theater, dancing, sculpting, painting

3. How did people become government officials?
   by passing a difficult exam

4. Why did the government take a census?
   to determine the empire's population

5. Why did trade in the Tang period flourish?
   New roads and waterways made travel easier.

CD-104308 • © Carson-Dellosa

Name _____

Read the story. Then, answer the questions.

The Silk Road

The Silk Road was not really a road, nor was it made out of silk. The Silk Road is the name used to refer to the route leading from Asia to the West. People traveled along this route to trade goods, including silk and spices from China and gold and silver from Rome, Italy. Few people traveled the entire distance of the Silk Road because it was several thousand miles long and very dangerous. The route included deserts and mountains, and there was always the danger of meeting bandits. People traded with each other along the way and took goods with them to others farther along. In addition to goods, ideas and inventions were also traded along the Silk Road. Some technological innovations that travelers brought from Asia to the West included the magnetic compass and the printing press. The Italian adventurer Marco Polo was one of many travelers along the Silk Road.

1. What is the main idea of this story?
   (a.) Many goods and ideas were traded along the Silk Road.
   b. The Silk Road was long and dangerous.
   c. Marco Polo traveled along the Silk Road.

2. What was the Silk Road?
   the route from Asia to the West along which goods were traded

3. What did people trade along the Silk Road?
   silk, spices, gold, silver, ideas, inventions

4. Why did few people travel the entire distance of the Silk Road?
   because it was too long and dangerous

5. What were two technological innovations brought from Asia to the West?
   magnetic compass, printing press

CD-104308 • © Carson-Dellosa

Name _____

Read the story. Then, answer the questions.

The Inca Empire

The Inca lived in the Andes Mountains in what is now Peru about 600 years ago. As the Inca empire expanded to include new areas, engineers and workers from the capital city of Cuzco built roads that connected the empire. Government officials recorded the number of people and the amount of wealth in the new areas, and governors were appointed to oversee them. The millions of people living in the Inca empire had to follow the Inca customs, including speaking the Incan language. Cuzco, which had gardens, paved streets, and stone buildings, was located high in the mountains. The city was used mostly for government work and for sending and receiving messages throughout the empire. The emperor and his family lived in Cuzco, but most other people were farmers in the countryside. Although the Inca were defeated by the Spanish in the 1530s, their descendants still live in Peru today.

1. What is the main idea of this story?
   a. The Spanish came to Peru in the 1530s.
   (b.) The Inca had an impressive empire about 600 years ago.
   c. Cuzco was the capital of the Inca empire.

2. What happened when a new area joined the Inca empire?
   Engineers built roads there, officials recorded the wealth and number of people, and a governor oversaw the area.

3. What did Cuzco look like?
   It had gardens, paved streets, stone buildings, and was located high in the mountains.

4. What activities took place in Cuzco?
   government work, messages sent and received

5. What did most people in the Inca empire do for work?
   They were farmers in the countryside.

CD-104308 • © Carson-Dellosa

Name _____

Read the story. Then, answer the questions.

The Trail of Tears

People of different cultures lived in North America before European explorers arrived. As Europeans began to settle the New World, they competed with Native Americans for land and other resources, such as gold. Over time, the New World was divided into states and a government was formed. The U.S. government passed laws in the 1830s making it legal to force Native Americans to relocate if settlers wanted their land. The Cherokee and other Native American groups had to move from the southeastern United States to lands farther west. Thousands of Native Americans traveled over 1,000 miles (1,600 kilometers) on foot from their homelands to the land that later became the U.S. state of Oklahoma. Many people died from disease or hunger along the route. The name "Trail of Tears" was given to this event in U.S. history because of the struggles people faced on their journeys. Today, the descendants of the survivors of the Trail of Tears make up the Cherokee Nation.

1. What is the main idea of this story?
   a. Many people from Europe settled in the New World.
   b. Some Native Americans still live in Oklahoma today.
   (c.) The Trail of Tears was a forced relocation of Native Americans in the United States.

2. What did European settlers compete with Native Americans for?
   land and resources, such as gold

3. How did the U.S. laws that were passed in the 1830s affect Native Americans?
   Many had to move from their homelands.

4. Where were Native Americans forced to move?
   the land that became the U.S. state of Oklahoma

5. What is the Trail of Tears?
   the relocation of Native American groups from their homelands to the land that became the state of Oklahoma

CD-104308 • © Carson-Dellosa

Read the story. Then, answer the questions.

The Vikings in Canada

The Vikings were the first Europeans to cross the Atlantic Ocean and reach North America. Historians knew that the Vikings settled in Greenland and Iceland but were not sure how much time they spent in Canada. In 1960, a Viking settlement from around 1000 A.D. was found at L'Anse aux Meadows, in what is now the Canadian province of Newfoundland and Labrador. Archaeologists uncovered the ruins of eight buildings that had sod walls and roofs over supporting frames. In the middle of each floor was a long, narrow fireplace used for heating and cooking. Archaeologists also found tools the Vikings had used. Because the design of the tools and the buildings was similar to those found in Viking settlements in Greenland and Iceland, it was clear that the Vikings settled in Canada as well. Today, L'Anse aux Meadows is a national historic site, and many people visit it each year.

1. What is the main idea of this story?
   a. A Viking group once lived in Canada at L'Anse aux Meadows.
   b. The first Europeans to reach North America were the Vikings.
   c. Many people visit national historic sites each year.

2. In which areas of North America did the Vikings settle?
   Greenland, Iceland, Canada

3. What was found in 1960 at L'Anse aux Meadows?
   a Viking settlement from around 1000 A.D.

4. What did the buildings at L'Anse aux Meadows look like?
   They had sod walls and roofs over supporting frames and long, narrow fireplaces.

5. How did archaeologists know that this was a Viking settlement?
   because the tools and buildings were similar to those found in Viking settlements in Greenland and Iceland

56   CD-104308 • © Carson-Dellosa

Read the story. Then, answer the questions.

The Klondike Gold Rush

The Klondike Gold Rush is named after a river where a large deposit of gold was found in 1896. The Klondike River is located near Dawson City in Canada's Yukon Territory. People who wanted to travel from Alaska into Canada in search of gold had to bring a year's worth of supplies with them because there were no places along the way to get more supplies. They often spent time in Edmonton, Canada, stocking up on food, tools, and clothing for the journey. The gold rush helped develop new towns in western Canada and the Pacific Northwest of the United States. In addition to thousands of prospectors, or people who searched for gold, the gold rush drew many professionals, such as doctors and teachers, who were needed in the new settlements. Today, the Klondike Gold Rush International Historical Park, which includes sites in both Canada and the United States, helps people remember the dreams of the prospectors and the difficulties they faced.

1. What is the main idea of this story?
   a. Only a few people became rich during the gold rush.
   b. The Klondike Gold Rush brought many new people to Canada.
   c. Dawson City is located in the Yukon Territory.

2. What is the Klondike Gold Rush named after?
   the Klondike River, where a large deposit of gold was found in 1896

3. What did people need to bring with them when traveling from Alaska to Canada?
   a year's worth of supplies

4. What did people often do in Edmonton?
   stock up on food, tools, and clothing

5. Where did new towns develop during the gold rush?
   western Canada and the Pacific Northwest of the United States

CD-104308 • © Carson-Dellosa   57

Read the story. Then, answer the questions.

North American Pioneers

Many early North American pioneers came from Europe. Some came to pursue religious freedom, while others wanted more land for their families. Many settlers built villages along the shores of lakes, rivers, or the ocean. Water was important not only for drinking, farming, and washing clothes, but for powering mills and traveling to other settlements. Most pioneers worked as farmers. They had to clear the land of trees before they could plant many crops. Pioneers also raised horses and oxen to help pull wagons, and sheep to provide wool. When there were enough children in a village, parents sometimes built a schoolhouse and hired a teacher. Usually, all of the children were taught in a single room. Otherwise, children might be educated at home. As villages grew in size, they sometimes built a doctor's office, a blacksmith's shop, and a general store where goods were sold.

1. What is the main idea of this story?
   a. Some pioneers came from Europe.
   b. Pioneer children sometimes studied at home.
   c. Most early pioneers were farmers who lived in small villages.

2. Why did the early pioneers come to North America?
   for religious freedom or more land

3. Which animals did pioneers often raise?
   horses, oxen, sheep

4. How were pioneer children educated?
   at home or in a single room in a schoolhouse

5. What other buildings might a pioneer village include?
   doctor's office, blacksmith's shop, general store

58   CD-104308 • © Carson-Dellosa

Read the story. Then, answer the questions.

New England

Six U.S. states make up the area of New England. Massachusetts was founded in 1630 by people who disagreed with the teachings of the Church of England. The first settlers there were the Pilgrims, who arrived on the *Mayflower* in 1620. Rhode Island was founded in 1636 by people who left the Massachusetts Bay Colony seeking religious freedom. People who settled in New Hampshire, which was founded in 1638, were looking for a place to fish and trade successfully. People who moved to Connecticut, which was founded in 1636, settled on the fertile farmland along the Connecticut River. Maine was once part of the Massachusetts Bay Colony but became a separate state under the Missouri Compromise of 1820. Vermont, founded in 1777, was fought over by several colonies and was originally called New Connecticut. Today, New England is famous for many things, including its beautiful autumn foliage and its fishing industry.

1. What is the main idea of this story?
   a. Many people in New Hampshire enjoy fishing.
   b. Massachusetts was founded in 1630.
   c. New England is a region of the United States.

2. Which states make up the area of New England?
   Massachusetts, Rhode Island, New Hampshire, Connecticut, Maine, Vermont

3. Why did people settle in Massachusetts and Rhode Island?
   religious freedom

4. What businesses did people in New Hampshire work in?
   fishing and trading

5. What is New England famous for today?
   its beautiful autumn foliage and its fishing industry

CD-104308 • © Carson-Dellosa   59

Reading about History

Read the story. Then, answer the questions.

Early Industries in North America

One of the earliest industries in North America was the trade of animal fur. Many French explorers who came to the New World in the early 1500s began to trade European goods, such as tools and jewelry, to Native American groups for animal pelts. The French traded furs and other goods around the lakes and rivers of North America. Another important industry was logging. Early settlers of North America had to chop down trees to make room for their farms. In addition to using logs for their own houses, fuel, and furniture, they sold wood to people in other areas to use for paper or durable goods. As farms grew successful, settlers also began to sell goods such as grain and rice. Another important industry in North America was mining. Settlers from Europe found that the New World had many natural resources to mine, such as gold, silver, and precious stones.

1. What is the main idea of this story?
   a. Many settlers used logs to build their houses.
   (b) Early North American industries included the fur trade, logging, and mining.
   c. Some early industries are still important today.

2. When did the French explorers come to the New World?
   in the early 1500s

3. Where did the French trade furs and other goods?
   around the lakes and rivers of North America

4. What goods did settlers begin to sell to people in other areas?
   wood, grain, and rice

5. What natural resources did settlers mine in North America?
   gold, silver, and precious stones

Reading about History

Read the story. Then, answer the questions.

The Panama Canal

The Panama Canal is a human-made shipping channel that connects the Pacific Ocean with the Atlantic Ocean. This waterway makes it much easier for ships to take goods from one place to another. Instead of traveling around the southern tip of South America, ships can cut through the Isthmus of Panama. An isthmus is a narrow strip of land that connects two larger landmasses and has water on its other sides. The Panama Canal was completed in 1914, after 34 years of effort by France and the United States. An estimated 80,000 people worked on the canal before it was completed. The canal works by opening a series of locks, or chambers, through which a ship passes. As the ship enters each lock, the water level slowly rises so that it can safely travel into the next area. Since the canal was built, over 800,000 ships have crossed through it.

1. What is the main idea of this story?
   (a) The Panama Canal is a waterway connecting two oceans.
   b. Panama is a country in South America.
   c. Many people worked on the canal before it was completed.

2. How did the Panama Canal change the way ships travel?
   Ships can now cross the Isthmus of Panama instead of traveling around the tip of South America.

3. What is an isthmus?
   a narrow strip of land connecting two landmasses that has water on its other sides

4. How long did it take to build the Panama Canal?
   34 years

5. What do ships pass through on the Panama Canal?
   locks or chambers

Reading about History

Read the story. Then, answer the questions.

The Smithsonian Institution

The Smithsonian Institution in Washington, D.C., is the largest museum complex in the world. The Smithsonian is named after James Smithson, a British scientist who wanted to create a research institution in the United States. The first structure in the museum complex was built in 1855. Today, the Smithsonian includes 19 museums, nine research centers, and the National Zoo. The National Museum of Natural History has exhibits on plants, animals, human cultures, gems, and ecosystems. The National Air and Space Museum has exhibits on the history and future of flight. The National Zoo has examples of habitats from around the world and works to educate people about protecting wild animals. The Smithsonian also has separate museums devoted to African art, sculpture, portraits of American leaders, folk art and photography, and Native American cultures. An estimated 24 million people visit the Smithsonian each year to see over 136 million objects.

1. What is the main idea of this story?
   a. The first structure in the Smithsonian system was built in 1855.
   (b) The Smithsonian is a large museum complex in the United States.
   c. Museums often have exhibits about human cultures.

2. Who is the Smithsonian named after?
   James Smithson, a British scientist

3. How many buildings does the Smithsonian include?
   29: 19 museums, 9 research centers, and the National Zoo

4. What type of exhibits does the National Air and Space Museum have?
   exhibits on the history and future of flight

5. What other subjects are Smithsonian museums devoted to?
   Answers will vary but may include African art, sculpture, portraits, folk art and photography, and Native American cultures.

Reading about Science

Read the story. Then, answer the questions.

Photosynthesis

Photosynthesis is the process in which plants use sunlight to produce food and oxygen. In addition to light, plants need water and carbohydrates to grow. A plant gathers water through its roots. It also takes in carbon dioxide from the air. A compound called chlorophyll helps plants use sunlight. Chlorophyll is what makes plants green. Plants use energy from the sun to break down the water and carbon dioxide. Through photosynthesis, plants produce oxygen and glucose. Glucose is a type of sugar that plants use for energy. Some people refer to trees as the "lungs of the planet." This is because trees help keep a balance between oxygen and carbon dioxide in the air. When people or animals breathe in oxygen, they exhale carbon dioxide. Plants convert carbon dioxide into oxygen that people and animals can breathe.

1. What is the main idea of this story?
   a. People and animals breathe in oxygen.
   b. Plants use energy from the sun.
   (c) Photosynthesis is a process that helps plants produce food and oxygen.

2. What do plants need to grow?
   light, water, carbohydrates

3. What makes plants green?
   chlorophyll

4. What is glucose?
   a sugar that plants use for energy

5. Why are trees sometimes called the "lungs of the planet"?
   because trees convert carbon dioxide into oxygen that people and animals can breathe

---

Name _____

Read the story. Then, answer the questions.

Migration

Some animals migrate, or move, to different areas during different seasons. They may go to warmer climates during the winter and cooler climates during the summer. Some whales swim to Hawaii in the autumn to give birth to their young in warm waters. Then, they travel to Alaska in the summer. Salmon begin their lives in freshwater streams and travel to the ocean as adults. Their bodies change so that they can survive in saltwater. When it is time to lay eggs, salmon swim back to the freshwater streams where they were born. Monarch butterflies fly thousands of miles every autumn, from the northern United States to Mexico. In the spring, they fly north again. Many birds also migrate every year. The arctic tern has the farthest journey, traveling over 22,000 miles (32,000 km) from the Arctic Circle at the North Pole to Antarctica at the South Pole.

1. What is the main idea of this story?
   - (a.) Some animals migrate at different seasons of the year.
   - b. The arctic tern migrates over 22,000 miles a year.
   - c. Hawaii has warmer waters than Alaska.

2. List one reason why animals might migrate.
   Answers will vary.; giving birth in warmer waters or laying eggs

3. Where do salmon travel during their lives?
   from freshwater streams to the ocean and back

4. Where do monarch butterflies migrate every autumn?
   from the northern United States to Mexico

5. Which animal has the farthest migration each year?
   the arctic tern

CD-104308 • © Carson-Dellosa

Name _____

Read the story. Then, answer the questions.

Fossils

Fossils are the remains of plants or animals from thousands of years ago that have turned to stone. After these organisms died, their bodies were buried in sediment and gradually replaced by minerals. Sometimes an animal's bones, teeth, or shell are preserved. Other times only an impression of its body is made. Footprints, eggs, and nests can also be fossilized. Fossils can be found in many places. They are often uncovered when people dig up the earth as they build roads. Many fossils are buried in layers of rock. Sometimes, fossils are exposed through erosion of a mountainside. Others are found through undersea excavation. Scientists study fossils to learn what the living animals or plants looked like. They can use radiocarbon dating to find out how old a fossil is. All living things contain carbon, so scientists measure how much carbon is left in a fossil to determine its age.

1. What is the main idea of this story?
   - a. Fossils can be found in many places.
   - b. Sometimes only an impression of a plant is left.
   - (c.) Fossils are plant or animal remains from long ago.

2. What happens when something is fossilized?
   Its body is gradually replaced by minerals.

3. What parts of an animal's body might be preserved?
   bones, teeth, or shell

4. Why do scientists study fossils?
   to learn what the living animals or plants looked like

5. How does radiocarbon dating help scientists determine a fossil's age?
   Scientists measure how much carbon is left in a fossil to determine how old it is.

CD-104308 • © Carson-Dellosa

Name _____

Read the story. Then, answer the questions.

Types of Rocks

Rocks are divided into three types, depending on how they were formed. These three types are igneous, sedimentary, and metamorphic. Igneous rocks are made when volcanoes erupt and release melted material called magma. After the magma cools, it forms solid igneous rock. One type of igneous rock is granite, a very hard material that is often used in construction. Sedimentary rocks form when water deposits sediments, or small pieces of rocks and sand. Over time, the sediments are compressed and form layers, forming sedimentary rock. One type of sedimentary rock is limestone, which often contains fossils and shells. Metamorphic rocks are the least common of the three types. Metamorphic rocks begin as igneous or sedimentary rocks but are squeezed tightly within the earth's crust over a long period of time. Marble is one type of metamorphic rock.

1. What is the main idea of this story?
   - a. Hard rocks can be useful for building sturdy structures.
   - (b.) There are three types of rock that are formed in different ways.
   - c. Not all rocks look the same.

2. What are the three types of rock?
   igneous, sedimentary, metamorphic

3. How do igneous rocks form?
   Volcanoes release magma. When the magma cools, it becomes solid rock.

4. How do sedimentary rocks form?
   Water deposits sediments. Over time, the layers are compressed and become sedimentary rock.

5. How do metamorphic rocks form?
   Igneous or sedimentary rocks are squeezed tightly over time.

CD-104308 • © Carson-Dellosa

Name _____

Read the story. Then, answer the questions.

The Beaufort Scale

Wind speed can be measured in miles or kilometers per hour (mph or km/h). A British naval commander in the early 1800s invented a chart called the Beaufort scale to describe the weather using wind speed. Beaufort numbers range from 0 to 12. The number 0 indicates that there is almost no wind, the sea is flat, and the land is calm. In a moderate breeze (number 4), the wind travels at 13–18 mph (20–29 km/h), small waves are present, and small branches begin to move. In a gale (number 8), the wind is moving at 39–46 mph (63–75 km/h), the sea has fairly high waves with breaking crests, and twigs on trees are breaking. During a hurricane (number 12), the wind speed is at least 73 mph (118 km/h), the sea is completely white with foam and spray, and there is massive structural damage on land.

1. What is the main idea of this story?
   - a. Wind speed is a rate measured in distance over time.
   - (b.) The Beaufort scale describes weather using wind speed.
   - c. Hurricanes can be very destructive.

2. What does the number 0 on the scale mean?
   There is almost no wind, the sea is flat, and the land is calm.

3. Describe a moderate breeze on the Beaufort scale.
   wind speed 13–18 mph or 20–29 km/h, small waves present, small branches moving

4. What happens during a gale?
   wind speed 39–46 mph or 63–75 km/h, high waves with breaking crests, twigs on trees breaking

5. What is the wind speed during a hurricane?
   at least 73 mph or 118 km/h

CD-104308 • © Carson-Dellosa

Answer Key

Name _____ **Reading about Science**

Read the story. Then, answer the questions.

Bird Watching

Many people enjoy the hobby of bird watching. It is a pastime you can do in your own yard. If you put seeds in a bird feeder or hang a birdhouse, you are more likely to attract birds. You may notice that birds visit the feeder at certain times of day, or that different birds prefer different types of foods. You may see baby birds trying their wings as they leave the nest for the first time. Some people travel to other parts of the world to see birds that they cannot see at home. They may use binoculars to get a better look at birds perching in trees or flying overhead. Some people keep lists of the species of birds that they have seen. There are even contests to see who can spot the most different birds over a period of time!

1. What is the main idea of this story?
   a. Bird watching is a popular hobby that many people enjoy.
   b. Some birds like to eat seeds, while others like fruit.
   c. There are many different species of birds.

2. How can you attract more birds to your yard?
   Put seed in a bird feeder or hang up a birdhouse.

3. What are some things you might notice about birds in your yard?
   Answers will vary.; what the birds like to eat or how they develop over time

4. What do people use to help them see birds from a distance?
   binoculars

5. What kind of contest might a bird watcher participate in?
   a contest to see who can spot the most different birds

68   CD-104308 • © Carson-Dellosa

Name _____ **Reading about Science**

Read the story. Then, answer the questions.

Biomes of the World

Biomes are areas of land or water that share the same climate. Earth has several major biomes. Deserts receive little rain and have extreme temperatures. Forests receive more rain and have moderate temperatures. The trees in a deciduous forest lose their leaves every autumn. The trees in the taiga are mostly evergreens, many of which have needle-like leaves. Grasslands cover the most area of land on Earth. Rain is usually seasonal, so there is a dry season during which dust storms may be created. The tundra is located at very high elevations and near the North and South Poles. Few plants grow in the tundra, and the ground is permanently frozen. There are two types of aquatic biomes: marine and freshwater. Marine biomes cover about three-fourths of Earth's surface and include all of the world's oceans. Freshwater biomes are bodies of water such as lakes, rivers, and ponds.

1. What is the main idea of this story?
   a. Some biomes receive little rain.
   b. Deserts can be very hot or very cold.
   c. Earth has many different biomes.

2. What are biomes?
   areas of land or water that share the same climate

3. How are deserts and forests different?
   deserts—little rain, extreme temperatures, forests—more rain, moderate temperatures

4. What do many evergreens look like?
   Many of them have needle-like leaves.

5. What happens during the dry season in the grasslands?
   Dust storms may be created.

CD-104308 • © Carson-Dellosa   69

Name _____ **Reading about Science**

Read the story. Then, answer the questions.

Energy Conservation

Conserving energy means being careful about how much energy you use and trying to use less energy. You can conserve energy by using cars with higher fuel efficiency, which means you can travel farther using less fuel. You can recycle or reuse materials, such as plastic, glass, paper, and metal, and you can buy products made from recycled materials. You can also conserve energy by using less at home. Wear heavier clothing instead of turning up the heat when the weather grows cooler. Turn off the lights when you leave a room and unplug small appliances and machines such as televisions and computers when you will be away from the house for a long period of time. Using less electricity, gas, and water means you will have lower utility bills and will help the environment.

1. What is the main idea of this story?
   a. Some materials can be recycled instead of thrown away.
   b. Utility bills are sometimes higher in the summer.
   c. There are many ways to conserve energy.

2. What does energy conservation mean?
   being careful about how much energy you use and trying to use less energy

3. Why might you want to use a car with high fuel efficiency?
   You can travel farther using less fuel.

4. What are some materials that can be recycled?
   plastic, glass, paper, metal

5. What are two ways to conserve energy at home?
   Answers will vary.; wearing heavier clothes instead of turning up the heat, turning off lights, unplugging appliances when you will be away for a long period of time

70   CD-104308 • © Carson-Dellosa

Name _____ **Reading about Science**

Read the story. Then, answer the questions.

Microscopes

A microscope is a scientific tool that helps people to see very small things. By magnifying tiny objects many times, scientists can view intricate details. Hans and Zacharias Janssen produced a tube with magnifying lenses at either end in the late 1500s. Anton van Leeuwenhoek developed a single-lens microscope in the mid-1600s. He was the first person to describe bacteria that he saw under the microscope. Early microscopes could magnify objects only up to 20 or 30 times their size, but Leeuwenhoek's device could magnify up to 200 times. Today, scientists use compound microscopes that have multiple lenses to further magnify an image up to 1,000 times. In 1931, two German scientists invented the electron microscope, which can magnify up to one million times. This device directs a beam of electrons at a cell sample to form an image that is captured on a photographic plate.

1. What is the main idea of this story?
   a. Scientists have developed and improved microscopes over time.
   b. Bacteria can be seen under a microscope.
   c. Compound microscopes use multiple lenses.

2. What did the device produced by Hans and Zacharias Janssen look like?
   It was a tube with magnifying lenses at either end.

3. What was Leeuwenhoek able to describe for the first time?
   bacteria

4. How has magnification in microscopes changed over time?
   It has increased from 20 times an object's size to over one million times an object's size.

5. How does an electron microscope work?
   Electrons are directed at a cell, and the image formed is captured on a photographic plate.

CD-104308 • © Carson-Dellosa   71

---

120   CD-104308 • © Carson-Dellosa

Name _____

Read the story. Then, answer the questions.

Potential and Kinetic Energy

Energy is the ability to do work. Energy can be found in the forms of motion, sound, heat, and light. All energy can be classified as either potential or kinetic. Potential energy is stored for later use. Kinetic means "being active," and things using kinetic energy have moving parts. You might think of cogs moving in an engine, but electricity is also an example of kinetic energy because it involves the movement of electrons. Sound and sunlight are also kinetic. Energy can be changed from potential to kinetic. A ball resting at the top of a slope has potential energy. As soon as the ball begins to roll, the energy becomes kinetic. When you are sitting at your desk, you have the *potential* to move. You may store up energy, especially if you sit for a long time. When you begin moving, you become *kinetic*.

1. What is the main idea of this story?
   a. Energy can be either kinetic or potential.
   b. Energy can be found in many different forms.
   c. A group of runners has kinetic energy.

2. What is potential energy?
   energy that is stored for later use

3. What is kinetic energy?
   energy of something that has moving parts

4. How does energy change from potential to kinetic?
   When something changes from being at rest to moving, the energy changes from potential to kinetic.

5. What is an example of kinetic energy?
   Answers will vary.; electricity, cogs in an engine, sound, sunlight

---

Name _____

Read the story. Then, answer the questions.

Exploring Space

People have been fascinated by outer space for centuries. The first animals sent into space were fruit flies, which traveled on a U.S. rocket in 1947. Many countries sent monkeys into space to investigate how space travel might affect humans. A Russian dog named Laika became the first animal to orbit Earth in 1957. In 1961, the Russian cosmonaut Yuri Gagarin became the first person to travel into space. His spacecraft orbited Earth once and then landed. In 1969, the American astronaut Neil Armstrong became the first person to walk on the moon. The United States developed a space shuttle during the 1980s that could be used many times, like an airplane. Russia built a space station called *Mir* that was used for many years. Astronauts began assembling the International Space Station in 1998. This research station is a cooperative project among many countries, including the United States, Russia, Japan, Brazil, Canada, and 11 European countries.

1. What is the main idea of this story?
   a. People have always been fascinated by outer space.
   b. Space travel has improved greatly over the past several decades.
   c. *Mir* was a Russian space station.

2. Why did many countries send monkeys into space?
   to see how space travel might affect humans

3. Who was the first person to travel into space?
   Yuri Gagarin

4. What was significant about the space shuttle?
   It could be used many times and is like an airplane.

5. What is the International Space Station?
   a research station that many countries are cooperating to build

---

Name _____

Read the story. Then, answer the questions.

Constellations

Constellations are patterns of stars that are present in the night sky. Some constellations are named after animals, and others are named after mythical characters. Although stars in a constellation may look close together, they are actually very far apart. Brighter stars are closer to Earth, and dimmer stars are farther away. The International Astronomical Union (IAU) recognizes 88 official constellations. One of the best-known constellations is the Big Dipper. The stars appear to form the handle and bowl of a water dipper. The Big Dipper is part of a larger constellation known as Ursa Major, or the Great Bear. People in different parts of the world see different constellations. Different constellations are also visible at different times of year. However, some constellations can be seen by people in both hemispheres. For example, the constellation of Orion, the hunter, is visible in both the Northern and Southern Hemispheres, but in the Southern Hemisphere it appears upside down!

1. What is the main idea of this story?
   a. Constellations are patterns of stars that are present in the night sky.
   b. Some stars are very far from Earth.
   c. Australia is located in the Southern Hemisphere.

2. What are constellations named for?
   animals or mythical creatures

3. Why do some stars appear brighter than others?
   Brighter stars are closer to Earth; dimmer stars are farther away.

4. What is the IAU?
   International Astronomical Union

5. What do the stars of the Big Dipper appear to form?
   the handle and bowl of a water dipper

Name _____

Read the story. Then, answer the questions.

Eclipses

An eclipse happens when Earth and the moon line up with the sun. A lunar eclipse occurs when Earth moves between the sun and the moon. Earth blocks some sunlight from reaching the moon, so the moon appears dark from Earth's shadow. A solar eclipse occurs when the moon moves between Earth and the sun. The moon blocks some sunlight from reaching Earth, so the sky grows dark. It is safe to view a lunar eclipse, but you should never look directly at a solar eclipse, even through sunglasses. Instead, make a pinhole projector. Cut a small square in the middle of a piece of cardboard. Place a piece of aluminum foil across it, and then poke a small hole in it so that the sun's light will shine onto another piece of cardboard. You can safely look at the sun's image on the second piece of cardboard.

1. What is the main idea of this story?
   a. You should never look directly at the sun.
   b. An eclipse happens when sunlight is blocked by Earth or the moon.
   c. The sky grows dark during a solar eclipse.

2. When does a lunar eclipse occur?
   when Earth moves between the sun and moon and blocks some sunlight from reaching the moon

3. What does the moon look like during a lunar eclipse?
   It is dark from Earth's shadow.

4. When does a solar eclipse occur?
   when the moon moves between Earth and the sun and blocks some sunlight from reaching Earth

5. How can you safely look at a solar eclipse?
   with a pinhole projector

Page 76 — Reading about Science

Name _____

Read the story. Then, answer the questions.

Human-Made Satellites

A satellite is an object that orbits around another object. The moon is a natural satellite of Earth. There are also many human-made satellites orbiting Earth. People use satellites to communicate, track the weather, gather environmental data, plot accurate global positions, and conduct research. The first satellite, called *Sputnik*, was launched by Russia in 1957. *Sputnik* sent signals back to Earth for 22 days, until its transmitter ran out of power. The first U.S. satellite, called *Explorer*, was sent into space in 1958. Satellites can be launched either with a rocket or with the space shuttle. Today, over 2,000 satellites are orbiting Earth. Some people think there are too many satellites in space. It is very costly to bring them back to Earth, so when they stop working, they usually stay in orbit. If their orbit is very low, they may reenter Earth's atmosphere and burn up.

1. What is the main idea of this story?
   a. The first satellite was launched in 1957.
   b. Some people think there are too many satellites in space.
   (c.) Satellites orbit around other objects and can be natural or human-made.

2. What is a natural satellite of Earth?
   the moon

3. What do people use satellites for?
   communicating, tracking weather, gathering environmental data, plotting global positions, conducting research

4. When was the first U.S. satellite sent into space?
   1958

5. How are satellites launched?
   with a rocket or with the space shuttle

76   CD-104308 • © Carson-Dellosa

Page 77 — Reading about Social Studies

Name _____

Read the story. Then, answer the questions.

Primary and Secondary Sources

When you conduct research for a paper, you use sources. A primary source may be a letter, a diary, an interview, a speech, or a law. Primary sources provide firsthand information about an event from the view of someone who was writing when the event occurred. A secondary source may be an encyclopedia or a textbook, which collect and interpret information from other sources after an event has happened. If you look at the last page in an encyclopedia entry, you may see a list of articles and books that the author has consulted. A letter written home from a soldier serving in World War II is a primary source. It might tell about his experiences with other soldiers in a foreign country. A book that examines the role of the United States during World War II is a secondary source. It might discuss several soldiers' letters and draw conclusions from them.

1. What is the main idea of this story?
   a. A textbook is a secondary source.
   b. Primary sources are written by someone present at an event.
   (c.) Research includes the use of both primary and secondary sources.

2. What kind of information do primary sources provide?
   firsthand information about an event

3. What does a secondary source do?
   collect and interpret information from other sources after an event occurs

4. What might an encyclopedia entry include on its last page?
   a list of articles and books that the author consulted

5. Give an example of a primary source you might use to write a paper about the Klondike Gold Rush.
   Answers will vary.

CD-104308 • © Carson-Dellosa   77

Page 78 — Reading about Social Studies

Name _____

Read the story. Then, answer the questions.

The Canadian Prime Minister

The Canadian prime minister leads Canada's federal government. Although the prime minister is head of the government, the British monarch is head of the country. Before being elected, the prime minister must first become the leader of his or her political party. The leader of the party that wins the most seats in Parliament, the legislative body of the federal government, becomes the prime minister. Most of the prime ministers of Canada have been lawyers, but some have been business leaders, teachers, and doctors. The prime minister chooses a cabinet of advisors to help make important policy decisions. Leaders of the provinces, called premiers, often meet with the prime minister to discuss what is best for the people living in the provinces. The prime minister must also work with leaders from other countries to discuss issues that affect Canada and the world.

1. What is the main idea of this story?
   (a.) The Canadian prime minister leads the federal government.
   b. Some prime ministers work in other careers prior to being elected.
   c. The prime minister must sometimes meet with foreign leaders.

2. What is the role of the British monarch in the Canadian government?
   head of the country

3. How is the prime minister elected?
   He or she becomes the leader of a political party, and the leader of the party winning the most seats in Parliament becomes prime minister.

4. What are some jobs that prime ministers have held before being elected?
   lawyers, business leaders, teachers, doctors

5. What role does the cabinet play in the government?
   It helps advise the prime minister on policy decisions.

78   CD-104308 • © Carson-Dellosa

Page 79 — Reading about Social Studies

Name _____

Read the story. Then, answer the questions.

U.S. Presidential Elections

The people of the United States choose a new president every four years. This election takes place on the first Tuesday after the first Monday in November. Presidential candidates must be at least 35 years old and be native U.S. citizens. Before the general election in November, people in different U.S. states hold elections to determine each party's candidates. These state-level party elections are called primaries and caucuses. A primary is a lot like a regular election because people go to the polls to vote. At a caucus, people meet to discuss the candidates and then nominate the one they choose. After the state-level elections, the political parties hold national conventions to nominate and confirm their candidates. Each presidential candidate chooses a running mate for vice president and then begins campaigning around the country. After the election, the new president is sworn into office on January 20 of the next year.

1. What is the main idea of this story?
   a. Candidates campaign to be president for many months.
   (b.) The U.S. president is chosen through a series of state and national elections.
   c. A vice president must serve if something happens to the president.

2. What are the requirements to become the U.S. president?
   at least 35 years old and a native U.S. citizen

3. What happens during a state primary?
   People go to the polls to vote for a party's candidate.

4. What happens during a state caucus?
   People discuss the candidates and nominate the one they choose.

5. What happens at a national convention?
   The political parties meet to nominate and confirm their candidates.

CD-104308 • © Carson-Dellosa   79

Name _____

Read the story. Then, answer the questions.

Languages of Canada

Canada has two official languages: English and French. Because the Constitution lists these languages as official, all federal laws must be printed in both languages. Many other languages are also spoken in Canada, including Chinese, Spanish, and Arabic. There are also over 50 Aboriginal languages, or languages spoken by natives. One or two languages are more common in different provinces or geographical regions. In some more populous provinces, such as Ontario and British Columbia, a greater variety of languages are spoken. This may be because more immigrants from other countries live in these areas and bring their native languages to Canada. Each province may choose whether to designate an official provincial language. The official language of Quebec is French. It is the primary language for over 80 percent of the people who live there. A majority of the people in the province of Nunavut speak an Inuit language.

1. What is the main idea of this story?
   a. Most people in Canada speak either English or French.
   b. Over 50 Aboriginal languages are spoken in Canada.
   c. Canada has two official languages, but many others are also spoken in Canada.

2. Why must all Canadian federal laws be printed in both English and French?

   because the Constitution lists these as official
   languages

3. What are Aboriginal languages?
   a. languages spoken by native peoples
   b. languages spoken only in Nunavut
   c. languages that are not written down

4. Why might more languages be spoken in some provinces than in others?

   because more immigrants live in some areas than in
   others

5. What is the official provincial language in Quebec?

   French

Name _____

Read the story. Then, answer the questions.

Languages of the United States

Although most people in the United States speak English, the country does not have an official language. English is used for official documents, laws, and court decisions. However, some areas require publications to be printed in another language if there are many speakers of that language living there. Thirty states have adopted English as their official language. Only one state, Hawaii, is officially bilingual. This means that the state recognizes two official languages, English and Hawaiian. Many people in the U.S. states bordering Mexico speak both English and Spanish. Other states, such as Louisiana and Maine, have a large number of French speakers. Many Native American languages are spoken on reservations, areas of land managed by native groups such as the Navajo and the Seminole. Because the United States is a nation of many immigrants, some people are reluctant to declare only one official language.

1. What is the main idea of this story?
   a. The United States has no official language, but many languages are spoken in the United States.
   b. Most people in the United States speak English.
   c. Spanish and French are spoken in some U.S. states.

2. What are some official publications for which English is used?

   documents, laws, and court decisions

3. When might a publication need to be printed in another language?

   when many people living in a location speak a language
   other than English

4. Which two states have a large number of French speakers?
   Louisiana and Maine

5. What is a reservation?

   an area of land managed by a native group such as
   Navajo or Seminole

Name _____

Read the story. Then, answer the questions.

Becoming a Canadian Citizen

Until 1947, people living in Canada were considered citizens of Great Britain. That year, the Canadian government passed a Citizenship Act declaring that its people were Canadian citizens. For the first time, they were able to use Canadian passports rather than British passports. Today, about 150,000 people become Canadian citizens every year. First, they must become permanent residents. This is a special legal status that says that a person has been approved to live permanently in Canada. After three years, a permanent resident is eligible to apply for Canadian citizenship. The person must be able to speak either English or French and must not have committed a crime in the past three years. The person must also pass a citizenship test to show that he or she knows Canadian history, geography, and government. After passing the test, new citizens take an oath during a citizenship ceremony declaring their allegiance to the British monarch and to Canada.

1. What is the main idea of this story?
   a. Canadians used to be British citizens.
   b. Many immigrants move to Canada each year.
   c. People who want to become Canadian citizens must complete several steps.

2. What did the Citizenship Act of 1947 declare?

   that people living in Canada were Canadian citizens
   rather than British citizens

3. How many people become Canadian citizens each year?
   about 150,000

4. What does it mean to become a permanent resident of Canada?

   to be approved to live permanently in Canada

5. What do citizens state when taking the oath of citizenship?
   their allegiance to the British monarch and to Canada

Name _____

Read the story. Then, answer the questions.

Becoming a U.S. Citizen

The United States is sometimes called a melting pot because its people come from many different countries and cultures. People who are born in the United States or who are born to U.S. citizens living outside the country are automatically U.S. citizens. People born elsewhere who want to become citizens must live in the United States for a certain amount of time and pass a citizenship test. This process is called naturalization. Each year, more than 450,000 people become U.S. citizens. To become a citizen, a person must have lived in the United States legally for at least five years and be able to read, write, and understand English. He or she must also pass a test covering the government, history, and Constitution of the United States. After meeting the other requirements, a new citizen must take an oath of allegiance to the United States in a special ceremony.

1. What is the main idea of this story?
   a. People who want to become U.S. citizens must meet certain requirements.
   b. Most U.S. citizens' families originally came from other countries.
   c. Many people move to the United States every year.

2. Why is the United States sometimes called a melting pot?

   because its people are a blend of many different
   cultures

3. Which people are automatically U.S. citizens?

   people born in the United States or born to U.S.
   citizens living outside the country

4. How many people become U.S. citizens each year?
   more than 450,000

5. What are two requirements to become a U.S. citizen?

   Answers will vary.; live in the United States for at
   least five years, understand English, pass a test, take
   an oath of allegiance to the United States

Name _____

Read the story. Then, answer the questions.

International Women's Day

International Women's Day is held on March 8. The first International Women's Day was celebrated in several European countries in 1911. The holiday was originally intended to promote the right of women to vote, earn equal pay to men, and hold public office. Many labor groups in different countries held marches to show their support for safe working environments and better wages for women. Today, people celebrate women's achievements in these areas but recognize that there is still a lot of work to do. In some countries, the holiday is similar to Mother's Day, and women receive gifts and bouquets of flowers from their families. In other countries, communities hold parades, political rallies, leadership development sessions, and career workshops for women. The United States designates the month of March as Women's History Month. Canada celebrates International Women's Week, a week of activities in March that honor women.

1. What is the main idea of this story?
   a. Some groups work to promote equal rights for women.
   (b.) International Women's Day recognizes achievements by women.
   c. The first International Women's Day was held in 1911.

2. When is International Women's Day held?
   March 8

3. How is International Women's Day similar to Mother's Day?
   Both holidays honor women. On these days, women
   may receive gifts and flowers from their families.

4. What types of activities are held in some countries?
   parades, political rallies, leadership development
   sessions, career workshops

5. How does Canada honor women?
   with International Women's Week

Name _____

Read the story. Then, answer the questions.

Labor Day

Labor Day is a U.S. holiday celebrated on the first Monday in September. This day honors the achievements of U.S. workers. Labor Day was first celebrated in 1882 in New York City, New York, when the Central Labor Union held a public demonstration and a picnic. By 1894, over half of the U.S. states had adopted the holiday. Later that year, the U.S. Congress passed a law making Labor Day a federal holiday. Many communities hold parades on Labor Day to demonstrate the variety of different services that workers provide. Community leaders and government officials sometimes give speeches in support of workers' rights. Labor Day marks the end of summer because city swimming pools often close after this day, and many children return to school. People in Canada and the United States celebrate Labor Day on the same day, but many other countries celebrate International Workers' Day on May 1.

1. What is the main idea of this story?
   a. Many people hold parades on Labor Day.
   (b.) Labor Day honors the achievements of workers.
   c. Sometimes families have picnics on Labor Day.

2. When is Labor Day celebrated?
   on the first Monday in September

3. What happened on the first Labor Day?
   The Central Labor Union held a public demonstration
   and a picnic in New York City.

4. When was Labor Day made an official U.S. federal holiday?
   1894

5. Which people might give speeches on Labor Day?
   community leaders and government officials

Name _____

Read the story. Then, answer the questions.

Rural Communities

Rural communities are areas where few people live and there are not many large buildings. Rural residents may live on farms or in small towns. Rural schools are often smaller than those found in cities. There may be only one high school instead of several. Students who attend rural schools probably know each other better because they share many classes with each other. People in rural communities may need to rely on people living near them when the weather is bad. They may also pool resources so that the whole community helps out when one family needs assistance. Many people in rural areas enjoy riding horses or taking long walks in the countryside. They also enjoy the nature that exists around them. Some urban residents like to visit rural areas to escape the hustle and bustle of the city.

1. What is the main idea of this story?
   a. Rural towns are often very small.
   b. Rural residents often enjoy being outside in nature.
   (c.) Rural areas have few people or buildings.

2. How are rural schools different from those found in cities?
   They are smaller, and there may be only one high
   school instead of several.

3. What is one advantage to living in a rural area?
   Answers will vary.; know students or neighbors better,
   help each other

4. What activities might people in rural areas enjoy?
   Answers will vary.; riding horses or taking walks in the
   countryside

5. Why do some urban residents like to visit rural areas?
   to get away from the hustle and bustle of the city

Name _____

Read the story. Then, answer the questions.

Urban Communities

People who live in cities live in urban communities. They may live in houses or in apartment buildings. Urban residents often have less space than people who live in the countryside. They may ride a bicycle or use public transportation instead of driving a car. Many cities have excellent bus, train, or subway systems. Urban schools may have several hundred students in each grade. They may also offer a greater number of activities, such as sports teams and special clubs, as well as classes to prepare students for college. Many cities have public areas like parks and swimming pools that their residents can enjoy together. They may also have community programs like children's afterschool activities or luncheons for elderly people. Cities require many government workers to run smoothly. In urban communities, people must learn to work together.

1. What is the main idea of this story?
   (a.) Urban communities have many people who share a small amount of space.
   b. People in cities sometimes do not have cars.
   c. Urban residents may enjoy a variety of activities.

2. How might people in urban communities get to work or school?
   by bicycle or public transportation, such as the bus,
   train, or subway

3. What are some urban schools like?
   They may have several hundred students per grade
   and may offer a greater number of activities.

4. Which public areas might urban residents enjoy together?
   parks and swimming pools

5. What kinds of community programs might a city have?
   Answers will vary.; children's afterschool activities or
   luncheons for elderly people

Name _____

Read the story. Then, answer the questions.

Demographics

Demographics are characteristics of human populations. The word *demographics* contains the root words *demo*, meaning "people," and *graph*, meaning "to write." Demographic data includes people's ages, occupations, educational levels, and income levels. Government officials can use this information to determine the makeup of a city or country's population, and whether there is a need for different services. If a city's officials learn that there are a great number of senior citizens, they may recommend building a retirement center. If they learn that many families with young children are moving into the area, they may recommend building additional schools. One way that countries collect demographic data is by taking a national census. In the United States, an official census of the population is taken every 10 years. In Canada, a national census is taken every five years. Both countries use demographics to examine trends in their populations.

1. What is the main idea of this story?
   a. Rural cities may have fewer residents than urban ones.
   b. Some cities have a large number of young people.
   ⓒ Demographics includes different kinds of information about people's lives.

2. What root words does *demographics* contain?
   demo, meaning "people," and graph, meaning "to write"

3. What types of information might demographic data include?
   people's ages, occupations, educational levels, and income levels

4. How do countries collect demographic data?
   through a national census

5. How often are censuses taken in the United States and Canada?
   United States—every 10 years, Canada—every five years

88   CD-104308 • © Carson-Dellosa

Name _____

Read the story. Then, answer the questions.

Coins and Cultures

Coins often show symbols of the cultures that produced them. Some ancient Greek coins had pictures of lions, geese, owls, turtles, or horses. Ancient Roman coins often included pictures of family members of the emperor. Their faces were shown in profile, or facing to the side. Coins in the United States do not have images of living people. On one side, a coin usually shows a famous U.S. president, and on the other, it usually shows a government building such as the Lincoln Memorial. The Canadian dollar coin, called the loonie, has a picture of a bird called a loon, which lives in areas of Canada. Other Canadian coins, including the penny, nickel, dime, and quarter, have pictures of Queen Elizabeth, the ruler of Great Britain, on one side. The other side of each coin shows an important symbol of Canada, including the maple leaf, the beaver, and the caribou.

1. What is the main idea of this story?
   ⓐ Coins show symbols of the culture that produced them.
   b. Some coins have images of people on them.
   c. The maple leaf is an important symbol of Canada.

2. What animals were shown on ancient Greek coins?
   lions, geese, owls, turtles, horses

3. What did ancient Roman coins often show?
   family members of the emperor

4. What do most Canadian coins show?
   Queen Elizabeth

5. How are U.S. coins different from Canadian coins?
   U.S. coins do not show images of living people. U.S. coins show government buildings instead of images from nature.

CD-104308 • © Carson-Dellosa   89

Name _____

The main idea of a paragraph tells what that paragraph is about. The other sentences in the paragraph give details that support the main idea. In the paragraph below, the sentences are out of order. Put the sentences in the correct order so that the paragraph makes sense. Begin with the sentence that states the main idea.

Writing a Paper

Finally, publish your paper.
Fourth, proofread your paper for errors in spelling and grammar.
First, think about what you would like to write.
Make some notes about what you will write.
This is the stage where you change any words or ideas so that your paper will make more sense.
Third, make your paper better by revising it.
Share your finished paper with your friends and family.
Second, write a rough draft.
A draft is an early version of your paper that helps you develop your ideas.
There are five steps to writing a paper.

There are five steps to writing a paper.
First, think about what you would like to write.
Make some notes about what you will write.
Second, write a rough draft.
A draft is an early version of your paper that helps you develop your ideas.
Third, make your paper better by revising it.
This is the stage where you change any words or ideas so that your paper will make more sense.
Fourth, proofread your paper for errors in spelling and grammar.
Finally, publish your paper.
Share your finished paper with your friends and family.

90   CD-104308 • © Carson-Dellosa

Name _____

The main idea of a paragraph tells what that paragraph is about. The other sentences in the paragraph give details that support the main idea. In the paragraph below, the sentences are out of order. Put the sentences in the correct order so that the paragraph makes sense. Begin with the sentence that states the main idea.

Making a Fruit Salad

Fourth, chill the fruit salad in the refrigerator until you are ready to eat it.
You might choose oranges, bananas, apples, and strawberries.
First, buy some fruit at a store.
The fruit should be cut into bite-sized pieces.
You can also buy yogurt to mix with the fruit.
Third, put the fruit pieces into a large bowl.
Second, ask an adult to help you cut the fruit.
Stir the yogurt into the fruit mixture.
Finally, enjoy your tasty snack!
Fruit salad is an easy and tasty recipe that you can make for your family.

Fruit salad is an easy and tasty recipe that you can make for your family.
First, buy some fruit at a store.
You might choose oranges, bananas, apples, and strawberries.
You can also buy yogurt to mix with the fruit.
Second, ask an adult to help you cut the fruit.
The fruit should be cut into bite-sized pieces.
Third, put the fruit pieces into a large bowl.
Stir the yogurt into the fruit mixture.
Fourth, chill the fruit salad in the refrigerator until you are ready to eat it.
Finally, enjoy your tasty snack!

CD-104308 • © Carson-Dellosa   91

Name _____ Main Idea and Sequencing

The main idea of a paragraph tells what that paragraph is about. The other sentences in the paragraph give details that support the main idea. In the paragraph below, the sentences are out of order. Put the sentences in the correct order so that the paragraph makes sense. Begin with the sentence that states the main idea.

Writing a Letter

You should write a salutation, or greeting, under the heading.
Then, write a closing to your letter.
You should write the heading at the top of the page.
Finally, write your signature so that the person will know who the letter is from.
The salutation begins with "Dear" and includes the name of the person to whom you are writing.
A letter has several important parts.
The closing includes words like "sincerely" or "yours truly."
The body includes the information you want to tell the person.
A heading includes your address and the date.
Next, you should write the body of the letter.

A letter has several important parts.
You should write the heading at the top of the page.
A heading includes your address and the date.
You should write a salutation, or greeting, under the heading.
The salutation begins with "Dear" and includes the name of the person to whom you are writing.
Next, you should write the body of the letter.
The body includes the information you want to tell the person.
Then, write a closing to your letter.
The closing includes words like "sincerely" or "yours truly."
Finally, write your signature so that the person will know who the letter is from.

CD-104308 • © Carson-Dellosa

Name _____ Main Idea and Sequencing

The main idea of a paragraph tells what that paragraph is about. The other sentences in the paragraph give details that support the main idea. In the paragraph below, the sentences are out of order. Put the sentences in the correct order so that the paragraph makes sense. Begin with the sentence that states the main idea.

Solving a Problem

Finally, check your answer to see if your idea worked.
If not, go back to an earlier step and try a new way of solving the problem.
Breaking the problem-solving process into steps can make it easier.
This can help you make sure that you understand the problem.
Second, brainstorm ways you could solve the problem.
First, state the problem in your own words.
Compare your ideas with the ideas of your friends to determine which idea will work the best.
Sometimes a problem can seem difficult to solve.
Make a list of the pros and cons of each idea.
Third, choose one way to try to solve your problem.

Sometimes a problem can seem difficult to solve. Breaking the problem-solving process into steps can make it easier. First, state the problem in your own words. This can help you make sure that you understand the problem. Second, brainstorm ways you could solve the problem. Compare your ideas with the ideas of your friends to determine which idea will work the best. Make a list of the pros and cons of each idea. Third, choose one way to try to solve your problem. Finally, check your answer to see if your idea worked. If not, go back to an earlier step and try a new way of solving the problem.

CD-104308 • © Carson-Dellosa

Name _____ Main Idea and Sequencing

The main idea of a paragraph tells what that paragraph is about. The other sentences in the paragraph give details that support the main idea. In the paragraph below, the sentences are out of order. Put the sentences in the correct order so that the paragraph makes sense. Begin with the sentence that states the main idea.

Writing a Book Report

First, choose a book to read.
Next, tell about the main character.
Finally, tell how the main character solved the problems.
While you are reading the book, take notes about the characters, setting, and plot.
Write the title of your book at the top of the page.
Writing a book report for a work of fiction can be easy if you break it into steps.
Start by describing the setting of the book.
At the end of your report, give your opinion of the book.
Then, write about the problems of the main character.
After you finish the book, you are ready to write your report.

Writing a book report for a work of fiction can be easy if you break it into steps. First, choose a book to read. While you are reading the book, take notes about the characters, setting, and plot. After you finish the book, you are ready to write your report. Write the title of your book at the top of the page. Start by describing the setting of the book. Next, tell about the main character. Then, write about the problems of the main character. Finally, tell how the main character solved the problems. At the end of your report, give your opinion of the book.

CD-104308 • © Carson-Dellosa

Name _____ Cloze

Missing Words

Read the story below. Every tenth word is missing. Fill in the blanks with the words from the word box below.

more	she	and	bike	broke
even	for	to	A	tighten
at	that	herself		

Lynne's friends had signed up for a bike race __at__ the end of the summer. Lynne had fixed her __bike__ many times, but she knew it was too old __and__ worn for the race. Lynne walked with her brother __to__ the bicycle shop. The owner, Mrs. Perriman, was looking __for__ someone to help fix bikes! Lynne told her how __she__ had helped her brother repair a flat tire and __tighten__ the brakes on his bike. She wanted to learn __more__ about how bicycles were put together. Mrs. Perriman said __that__ she had a job for Lynne at the race. __A__ good mechanic was needed to help cyclists whose bicycles __broke__ down along the route. Lynne thought that sounded like __even__ more fun than riding a bike in the race __herself__!

CD-104308 • © Carson-Dellosa

Worksheet (page 96)

Name _____

Cloze

Missing Words

Read the story below. Every tenth word is missing. Fill in the blanks with the words from the word box below.

she	classmates	there	new	office
A	her	the	third	to
her	of	and		

Angelica was nervous about going to middle school. Her **classmates** from her old school would make up only a **third** of the students in her grade. She knew that **there** would be more classes to find in different parts **of** the building. She would need to leave some of **her** books in her locker. Angelica's dad took her to **the** middle school to enroll her in the right classes. **A** friendly student named Kit smiled at her and offered **to** show her around. Kit showed Angelica the hall where **her** locker would be. Kit walked Angelica to the cafeteria **and** the gym. When they got back to the school **office**, Angelica's dad was waiting for her. Angelica told him **she** was no longer nervous because she would have a **new** friend on the very first day.

96   CD-104308 • © Carson-Dellosa

Worksheet (page 97)

Name _____

Cloze

Missing Words

Read the story below. Every eighth word is missing. Fill in the blanks with the words from the word box below.

grandfather	took	too	of	loves
Now	is	beach	learning	one
are	smell	was	visit	note
go	the			

Sharla and her family go to the **beach** every summer to visit their grandfather. He **is** a fisherman. When Sharla was small, she **was** afraid to get in the water. She **took** swimming lessons and surprised her grandfather by **learning** to swim before she visited him again. **Now**, Sharla's sister is learning to swim. Their **grandfather** wants them to be safe when they **visit** him. Everyone wears a life jacket in **the** boat. They check the weather before they **go** out on the ocean. They leave a **note** for Sharla's parents to tell where they **are** and when to expect them back. Sharla **loves** to visit the beach. She likes the **smell** of the saltwater and the golden shimmer **of** the sunlight on the water. She hopes **one** day she can live at the beach, **too**.

CD-104308 • © Carson-Dellosa   97

Worksheet (page 98)

Name _____

Cloze

Missing Words

Read the story below. Every eighth word is missing. Fill in the blanks with the words from the word box below.

play	said	the	with
music	similar	Aaron	the
There	director	called	could
times	the	which	choose

Aaron's aunt Sue played the clarinet in **the** orchestra. Aaron had seen her perform many **times**. Aunt Sue liked playing many kinds of **music**, from symphonies to jazz. Sometimes she played **with** a small group of only five players, **called** a chamber quintet. Aaron wanted to join **the** school band, but he was not sure **which** instrument he wanted to play. He liked **the** clarinet, but he was not sure he **could** play it as well as Aunt Sue. **There** were many other students who wanted to **play** the clarinet, so Aaron thought he should **choose** a different instrument to try. The band **director** asked Aaron to try playing the saxophone. **Aaron** loved the sound it made! Aunt Sue **said** that the clarinet and saxophone are very **similar**, so they could play duets together.

98   CD-104308 • © Carson-Dellosa

Worksheet (page 99)

Name _____

Cloze

Missing Words

Read the story below. Every fifth word is missing. Fill in the blanks with the words from the word box below.

creating	difficult	runner	mom	She	Jena
find	first	mom	will	morning	able
Jena	with	raise	Jena	help	around
through	by	run	to	adult	the
she	aware				

Jena's mom is a **runner**. She competes in races **around** the United States to **raise** awareness of diabetes. Jena's **mom** has diabetes but is **able** to control its effects **through** medicine, diet, and exercise. **She** rises early every morning **to** train for her races **by** running up and down **the** hills around their house. **Jena** often runs with her **mom**. She knows that by **creating** good habits today, she **will** be healthier as an **adult**. At first it was **difficult** to wake up to **run** before dawn, but now **she** looks forward to it. **Jena** loves feeling the cool **morning** air and spending time **with** her mom. Next summer, **Jena** will run in her **first** race. She wants to **help** her mom make others **aware** of the need to **find** a cure for diabetes.

CD-104308 • © Carson-Dellosa   99

Answer Key

Name _____

Compare and Contrast

Compare and Contrast

When you describe the similarities between people, things, or events, you compare them. When you describe their differences, you contrast them.

Read the following stories and think about the comparisons and contrasts in each. Then, answer the questions below each story.

Amphibians and reptiles are both cold-blooded animals. Both live in many different areas of the world. Reptiles have hard-shelled eggs, but amphibians have soft, sticky eggs. When reptiles hatch, they look like tiny adults. Amphibians go through several life stages as they grow older.

What two things are being compared in this story?

amphibians, reptiles

How are the two things similar? How are they different?

similar—both animals, cold-blooded, live in many areas; different—reptiles have hard eggs, but amphibians have soft, sticky eggs; reptiles look like adults when they hatch, but amphibians go through life stages

Books and newspapers are both things that people like to read. Books usually take more time to read because they are longer. Newspapers are published daily or weekly, while a book might be published only once. Newspapers tell about events in your community. Books tell about subjects that may be fictional, or made up by the author.

What two things are being compared in this story?

books, newspapers

How are the two things similar? How are they different?

similar—people like to read both; different—newspapers published daily or weekly, books published less often, are longer; newspapers tell about local events, and books tell about fictional subjects

100   CD-104308 • © Carson-Dellosa

Name _____

Compare and Contrast

Compare and Contrast

When you describe the similarities between people, things, or events, you compare them. When you describe their differences, you contrast them.

Read the following stories and think about the comparisons and contrasts in each. Then, answer the questions below each story.

Storks and parakeets are both birds. Storks have very long legs and long necks. They do not sing. Storks wade into water to find fish to eat. In contrast, parakeets are sometimes kept as pets. They have short bills and can sing. They can even learn to talk if trained. They eat flowers, fruit, and seeds.

What two things are being compared in this story?

storks, parakeets

How are the two things similar? How are they different?

similar—both birds; different—storks have long legs and necks, do not sing, and eat fish; parakeets are sometimes kept as pets, have short bills, can sing and learn to talk, and eat flowers, fruit, and seeds

Aquariums and planetariums both have exhibits. An aquarium has animals such as fish and turtles that live in the water. A planetarium displays objects having to do with space, including pictures taken by astronauts and rocks brought back from the moon. Both museums can be good places to learn new things.

What two things are being compared in this story?

aquariums, planetariums

How are the two things similar? How are they different?

similar—both have exhibits, good places to learn new things; different—aquarium has animals that live in water; planetarium has objects from space

CD-104308 • © Carson-Dellosa   101

Name _____

Compare and Contrast

Compare and Contrast

When you describe the similarities between people, things, or events, you compare them. When you describe their differences, you contrast them.

Read the following stories and think about the comparisons and contrasts in each. Then, answer the questions below each story.

Biographies and mysteries are both types of books. A biography tells facts about a person's life. It might be written by that person or by someone else. A mystery is usually fictional, or made up. It describes how a puzzle or problem is solved by a detective, a police officer, or another person.

What two things are being compared in this story?

biographies, mysteries

How are the two things similar? How are they different?

similar—both types of books; different—biography tells facts about someone's life and can be written by that person or someone else; mystery is usually made up and describes how a puzzle is solved

Stars and planets are both objects in outer space. They are both very far from Earth and look like bright specks in the night sky. A planet is solid, but a star is a ball of hot gases. Planets get light from the sun, while stars produce their own light. Stars are extremely hot, but planets can be any temperature.

What two things are being compared in this story?

stars, planets

How are the two things similar? How are they different?

similar—objects in outer space, far from Earth; different—planets are solid, light from sun; stars are gas, hot, make own light

102   CD-104308 • © Carson-Dellosa

Name _____

Compare and Contrast

Compare and Contrast

When you describe the similarities between people, things, or events, you compare them. When you describe their differences, you contrast them.

Read the following stories and think about the comparisons and contrasts in each. Then, answer the questions below each story.

Soccer and basketball are both sports played with a ball. Both are team sports that are played on a rectangular area. Soccer is played with the feet, while basketball is played with the hands. In soccer, the ball is kicked into a net, while in basketball, the ball is thrown through a hoop.

What two things are being compared in this story?

soccer, basketball

How are the two things similar? How are they different?

similar—both popular team sports played with a ball on a rectangular area; different—soccer is played with feet and the ball is kicked into a net; basketball is played with hands and the ball is thrown through a hoop.

Canada and the United States are both countries in North America. Canada is divided into provinces and territories, while the United States is divided into states. Canada is ruled by Parliament and the prime minister, while the United States has Congress and the president. Both countries have people who speak many different languages.

What two things are being compared in this story?

Canada, United States

How are the two things similar? How are they different?

similar—North America, different languages; different—Canada has provinces, ruled by Parliament and prime minister; United States has states, ruled by Congress and president

CD-104308 • © Carson-Dellosa   103

Congratulations!

receives this award for

_____

_____

Signed _____

Date _____

autobiography	amplify
© CD	© CD
abundant	abbreviate
© CD	© CD
buckle	bristle
© CD	© CD
brisk	beverage
© CD	© CD
chime	certificate
© CD	© CD
caption	campus
© CD	© CD
custom	confident
© CD	© CD
coax	circumstance
© CD	© CD

discard	demonstrate	deliberate
enchant	emphatic	distribute
exquisite	exhilarating	excel
former	fluid	flexible

dehydrate
distinguish
equivalent
faculty

glimmer	**glaze**	**gingerly**	**fragile**
© CD	© CD	© CD	© CD
hemisphere	**habitat**	**guarantee**	**grammar**
© CD	© CD	© CD	© CD
initial	**inhabit**	**immigrant**	**identical**
© CD	© CD	© CD	© CD
literal	**lavish**	**jostle**	**intention**
© CD	© CD	© CD	© CD

metropolitan	mechanism	maximum	manuscript
© CD	© CD	© CD	© CD
nerve	narrate	minimum	miniature
© CD	© CD	© CD	© CD
outlandish	occupation	nourish	neutral
© CD	© CD	© CD	© CD
plume	perceive	partially	paragraph
© CD	© CD	© CD	© CD

radiant	role	signature	supervise
quilt	retrieve	serene	speculate
query	respiration	scour	soar
quench	relay	schedule	skim

texture	thermometer	thrive	toll
tranquil	typical	unison	urgent
utensil	vacant	verge	vehicle
vicinity	vivid	wallet	wrench